JOE THOMPSON
Sleevenotes

POMONA

A Pomona Book

POM:30

Published by Pomona Books 2019
Suite 4
Bridge House
13 Devonshire Street
Keighley
West Yorkshire
BD21 2BH

www.pomonauk.com

A CIP catalogue record for this book
is available from the British Library

ISBN: 978-1-904590-35-4

Set in Linotype Granjon by Geoff Read
Design: www.geoffread.com

Cover image of Joe Thompson by Freddie Thompson

Mad in England!

Printed and bound by TJ International, England

Whatever you're meant to do, do it now.
The conditions are always impossible.

– Doris Lessing

CONTENTS

Introduction

This book, on the outside, is about some songs. Really though it's more the story of a band despite the songs. This band is not a big and successful band in the traditional sense. Time may not treat this band kindly. History may skip this musical chapter. Yet, the same as thousands of other bands, this one, for over a decade and a half, has run its course in a manner that has pleased the band's players. We've chosen this path.

There's an old tale of woe, it runs like this. A man goes to the big city because he's heard the streets are paved with gold. When he gets there, he realises three things. One, the streets are not paved with gold. Two, the streets are not paved at all. Three, it's his job to pave them.

This is true of music and most things in general. The moral being, you have to build your own world, choose the materials and create it to your satisfaction.

We've released a lot of records and played throughout Europe. We have jobs that have been bent and twisted to fit in. We have families and loved ones that are supportive and generous. This band is part of our life. We treat it seriously but not so much that it's the be all and end all. We've made hundreds of friends and a few enemies. We're not worried about our standing in the traditional music world. Getting on Radio One in the daytime is unlikely. Jools Holland won't have us on his radar. It's hard to explain sometimes. Maybe this book will help my mum understand. I'm pretty sure she has no idea what the hell has been going on. I'm going to try and write it without swearing. It will jump about. It will be....

messy.

The mighty @hey_colossus @mothclub tonight in both 6-piece and then 5-piece mode after technical issues, which led to a guitar going through an old Carlsbro amp, a Laney head getting tossed around and the fracturing of a Tele Deluxe's headstock all mid-song as the rest of the band played on. Great show, despite/as a result of, the madness.

– Instagram post by 'Tikierie'

It's our fifteenth anniversary show. *Fifteen years.* God knows. We're playing at The Moth Club in Hackney. The 'Memorable Order of Tin Hats', where the 'Moth' in 'Moth Club' comes from, is a meeting point for ex-military women and men. It's a club that is draped in 1950s and 1960s décor, has well-aged photographs on the walls from the 1970s and certainly contains a few smells from the early 1980s. Lady Gaga played here in 2016, secretly. It's now trendy, but the Memorable Order of Tin Hats still run the place. Their plaques and rules are all over the building. "All children off the dance floor after 9.30pm," and a more recent rule, "No smoking on the dance floor." You can somehow sense the begrudging tone on that last one. The dance floor is barely more than ten feet by ten feet. It's good to have rules for that sort of space.

We are four weeks into a scorched-earth heatwave. It hasn't dipped beneath twenty-four degrees. The grass is brown. They will be talking about this freak weather in years to come. I think we've finally trumped the heatwave of '76 that no one I know, apart from my parents, remembers. Gardeners hate this weather. I love the way it sepia tones our world in real life as if it's forcing a memory into us.

First off, the Somerset arm of Hey Colossus (HC) get into London early to co-host *The Baba Yaga Radio show* on Resonance FM. I've spent hours getting records together for it. Any excuse to go through the collection. Anthony Chalmers runs Baba Yaga. He's a promoter in London, and he's putting the show on tonight. This is his radio show, using it to help push his nights. I've never done this before and don't speak into the microphone for the first half of the show. People can't hear me, apparently. A message is passed on. I start yelling into the microphone. Then I play two records at the same time. All the while dripping sweat onto the records, onto the floor, onto Anthony. In case you're interested, I play: Brutal Knights, Zounds, The Chats, Ollie and Jerry, The Monkees, Baby Huey, The Marvelettes, Umoja, Nancy Dupree and Fugazi. Anthony plays some bands that he's soon to be putting on. The room is tiny. The room is hotter than outside. Then we go and get some lunch from Borough Market.

We're in Hackney in plenty of time to catch most of the France v Uruguay World Cup quarter-final before loading in and setting up. Then we're back out to catch most of the Brazil v Belgium match. The World Cup brings people together. It fills pubs. Football haters have been known to begrudgingly tuck in. There's no harm in it. I pretend to like tennis during Wimbledon. I pretend to like cricket during the Ashes. We all take one for the team occasionally.

There's a man with history etched into his face adjacent to our table. He's lived in Hackney for over forty years and has seen some changes. The bar staff know him and bring him pints when he gives the vaguest of glances bar-wards. From a young age this has been an ambition of mine, to be the vague glancer in a pub as I sit there telling people how it used to be. This will never happen. All the pubs will be closed by 2040. Maybe I'll stroll around town with a bag of energy drinks shouting at the kids on hover-boards, "I remember when it was all hostelries round here!" I will definitely use the word 'hostelry'. I'll want it to be known that I'm from a different time.

We're playing with Anthroprophh. They're from Bristol. They go on first. They release their records on the same label as us so it's a night where the majority in attendance should enjoy both bands. Consequently, most people are in the venue from the beginning. As it should be. Then we play. (Something that will make sense by the time you get to the end of all these words: the live records don't turn up on time).

There's an independent music website called *The Quietus*. I was asked to write some words for it:

> When Hüsker Dü signed to Warner in 1986, noted puritan Ian MacKaye of Fugazi observed that once-DIY bands signing major meant they were no longer 'confederates in the same conspiracy'. To talk about the term DIY in relation to how one acts with one's music is both personal, and a minefield. Once you step out of your bedroom shouting about your music you're arguably already one step away from being PURE DIY.

When we started our own label in the late 1990s we relied on bands doing shows to sell the records. Some did, and they sold well. Some didn't, and they didn't sell as well. The 1990s doesn't feel long ago but it's an age in the music world: we weren't streaming albums back then, and social media didn't exist. People were only just beginning to enjoy the benefits of mail order.

Considering the costs of recording and the ease of getting people to hear your music nowadays, I wonder if being DIY now is so common that its meaning has changed. The days of selling 500 LPs out the boot of your car, Sun Ra-style and surviving on it are fading. DIY is a flag being waved by so many artists that the original against-the-grain standing has gone.

It surprises many people that members of bands considered successful are also in full-time work, which personally I love. No one has a God-given right to make money from entertainment and, arguably, to make money you must sell a crucial part of what you do down the river.

Yet the structure of our world is so based around wealth. When I'm at work as a postman one of the first questions I get asked the morning after a gig is: "What money did you get?/ How much were you paid?/ Did you lose money?/ MONEYMONEYMONEY!" It's how most people judge success and failure. The band I do, with five friends, makes no money. Since beginning in 2003 we have made no money. Every single penny goes into recording and rehearsing and new strings and mending broken things. We all have jobs. We write and record music because it's fun. We're lucky enough to play shows throughout mainland Europe. We're delighted to drive to shows and play to 30 people or more if the weather is right/no other bands are in town/there's nothing on telly (these are the top three promoter excuses, straight from the handbook). Kind people will put the show on and feed us and let us stay in their houses or put us up in the venue. We've stayed in squats with no toilets or showers and we've stayed in surprisingly swanky hotels (spending the night pinching ourselves and taking photos like tourists), but both are greeted with open arms. Often the squat sticks in your mind for a longer time, often for positive reasons. This network, a spider's web, holds us up. It's built over time, handed down through the generations. Money is nothing to do with what we do, and the minute it has anything to do with what you create you're done for, you're a spent force. I look at big labels run by people I vaguely know. I know they have splendidly underground/interesting music tastes, but they can't get away with releasing what they want because it won't sell in the number required to keep their mortgages paid. It must crush them. It must be like working in a footwear factory and not being allowed to make those platform shoes with the goldfish in the soles that we all secretly want.

I have two teenage sons and they both love music yet neither of them has bought a single piece of music in his life. They don't need to. Music is seen as free, pouring out the internet geyser like Old Faithful, spurting a new mix of tracks or hurling up a 20-year-old Weezer album. I'm not sure I even knew they liked music until the older one (Stan) came downstairs one day and said: "Did you know Dave Mustaine was once in Metallica?" Time stood still and looking at him was like looking in a mirror 25 years ago. New music fans are buried in their rooms with headphones on. Houses are becoming silent as the family unit is spread over separate rooms all digging different sounds quietly. The generation that is growing up purely on the internet is getting older. The TV is becoming redundant and it won't be too long before stereos take their place next to the dusty Breville in the garage. The much-hyped vinyl revival is just so much hot air.

The flipside, of course, is belligerence and progress. In the UK, labels such as La Vida Es Un Mus still fly the flag for the punk-rock DIY route, and it's totally working. Bad Breeding, The Lowest Form (not on La Vida, but the drummer runs the label, the band moves in the same circles), Anxiety – all three are prime examples of UK bands who are travelling the seas, meeting people, playing shows and doing it the old-school way. They are using the tools available – streaming, Bandcamp. Vinyl prices are kept low. It's possible. UK hip hop acts such as 67 can get millions of YouTube streams with no physical product and seemingly no backing. Grime artists have re-defined ideas of DIY in recent years, creating their own world, building new systems. Acts such as Stormzy have broken through with a solid foundation of making money from way more channels than the old model of flogging records and tickets. Check the first 12 seconds of Wiley's 2017 'Speaker Box': 'There's no money that record labels can offer us no more..." He's right. Once upon a time record labels ran the industry. You signed to them and couldn't escape. It still amuses me when you read that so-and-so has appeared on a certain record 'courtesy of Geffen' or whoever. Those days are almost over, thankfully. The industry is trying to climb out of a hole that is getting deeper and deeper, and the ladders aren't long enough.

It's inspiring to see Sleaford Mods do it on a label run by

a bus driver (Harbinger Sound). It's inspiring to see labels run by music lovers who aren't tied up in the trad world and can release what they love, not caring too much as long as it comes close to breaking even.

On a personal level, in a band where all the members have jobs and in a world where family and life is on a level with music, the occasional victories that we achieve are all reasons to be doing it – playing a decent show, getting home without breaking down, releasing a new record, coming up with a new tune, meeting excellent people, getting a good review (or even a well-aimed terrible review), fluking a BBC 6 Music play, getting to the M&S on the A303 before they shut and picking up a reduced three-bean wrap, whatever. This shit is social, it's a shared experience. It's sitting round chatting about the state of the nation until 4am with the promoter in whatever town you're in. It's being in total control. I have absolute and total faith that the Sun Ra, press-your-own-records, fuck-em-all route to enlightenment will find a way in whatever future fashion. It's releasing records as frequently as you like without being told you have to tour for three years to promote it. it's changing the way you do things and learning better ways. It's not being worried about keeping to the same sound to make sure the label and fan base are comfortable. It's about improving yourself as a person and keeping your mind moving. It's about letting it seep into your normal life and letting the knowledge you pick up inform your everyday choices. If you have the utter conviction in what you're doing you can do very well. DIY as was is dead. But long live DIY.

A WITCH IS BORN

from Hey Colossus Hates You And You
And You And You And You And You And
You And You And You And You And You
2004

Our first show was with Trencher (a Casio Grind three-piece),
Southall Riot and a band called Thread, September 2003. The
night was put on by Victory Garden, a record label based out of
extreme West London. It was at The Buffalo Bar right next to
Highbury and Islington tube station. The venue has long gone;
it's now something more appropriate for the area. The city is
changing. The centre where the big money is, is spreading. They
can't be having anchors like music venues dragging it back. The
goodness is being squeezed further and further out. We've even
moved out. We now live in Somerset where little happens; our
main excitement is seeing whether the swallows come back and
live and breed in the same nest above our garage. Year after year,
they do. It's illegal to get rid of the nest, apparently, so we leave
it and wait. They are tough birds. They fly miles and miles to get
to their nest and spend three or four months breeding and eating
worms and shitting all over our walls, windows, van, car, drives
and onto our heads.

We moved out of Walthamstow. In the early twenty-first-
century nothing happened in Walthamstow. Now everyone I
know lives there and bands play there. The cinema has re-opened.
It's the happening place and I'm jealous. London squeezes the

population out like a tube of toothpaste. The full end is where the action is, the empty end is where it was. They now try and set up culture centres, not realising they moved the culture out and the only people left are people whose work is their lives. People who care not about anything other than Starbucks and going to the gym and making money and keeping money and wearing no socks. These folk are probably good at what they do, but they do not traditionally go to see an electronic noise side project conjured up by the Trencher keyboard player. So the keyboard player from Trencher moves his show to Walthamstow. It is what it is, and we the people always find a way.

Oh, in case you don't know what Casio Grind is, and it stuns me that you would be unaware of this, here's a briefing. It's a type of music where the little 1980s keyboard that the kids of that era had, squeals over the top of brutally fast distorted bass and blast-beat riddled technical hardcore drums. The singer would be performing all sorts of vocal gymnastics, singing about both grim and hilarious subjects while falling on the floor and crying. In the late 1990s and early 2000s there were literally tens of bands doing this, ranging from the successful like Melt Banana to the marginally successful, The Locust and Trencher, down to the few who put out limited split 5" records with Melt Banana, Trencher and The Locust. It was both funny and exhilarating and very brief. Fifteen-minute sets, people falling over, masks, edgy subject matter and Vice Magazine lapped it up. Seeing Trencher in Rough Trade, when it was beneath Slam City in Covent Garden, was my oldest son Stan's (then aged three) first ever show. I think he liked it. It was hard to tell. He did ask to leave but three-year olds ask to leave everything.

As an aside, I also saw PJ Harvey in the same Rough Trade around the release of the first album. God damn, that three-piece were good. This is in no way related to this book. Although later, if U2's lawyers will let me, I would love to tell a tale regarding a soon-to-be Colossus guitarist playing in Polly Harvey's band, a camera and Bono on a plane. I bet they won't. Any use of the letter U and number 2 is seriously monitored nowadays. Ask Negativeland who sampled a slice of the Irish band's song 'I Still Haven't Found What I'm Looking for' along with a splendidly cuss-riddled rant from US DJ Casey Kasem. The record label SST, run by Greg Ginn from Black Flag, who released it, almost went bust because of it. Of course, U2 soon went on to tour the world sampling and using voice clips from news pieces as part of their ZooTV performances. Thus proving, as if proof were ever needed, that the mainstream will always crush the underground while simultaneously lifting ideas from it.

HC started when Stanton stopped. Stanton was a band Bob Davis and I did, with Chris Thompson and Simon Hughes, from the mid 1990s through to 2003. We were initially a four-track, lo-fi affair, recording our songs onto a four-track machine, bouncing the tracks down, losing sound quality at each stage. We became a band with songs that we could all play. Bob and I have known each other since we were two. We went to playgroup together. I called for him on the way to school. We formed our first band when we were twelve and have now spent over thirty years in bands together. We are Lips and his mate from Anvil, we are the two from Status Quo. We are a couple of middle-aged men with kids and wives and whatnot. Chris was our seventh drummer. He is my brother. He had never played the drums before but was persuaded to buy a set and learn them. We were fed up of drummers leaving. The fourth person involved was Simon. We met at West Herts College. He's from Essex via Canada. He had boxes of cassettes that he'd recorded his songs on. He wrote hundreds of songs and talking about music over pints of Student Union-priced booze was the only highlight of being at that place.

Three years into the twenty-first-century, Chris moved to Brisbane with his wife Maggie. They were leaving behind their overpriced box flat in the East London suburb of Walthamstow, seven miles from the centre of the city. The flat's ceilings were a touch over the standard Thompson height of six-foot-four; there was no room for a Mohican. The windows being open let in the sensual ambience of a classic hectic city crossroad. Blackhorse Road Tube on one corner, the Standard Music venue on the other, cars howling past 168 hours a week. It was so loud the doors slammed. The underground train shook the flat's floors. The overground train running to Hackney from North London would thunder by, 'So often you won't notice' (copyright: Elwood Blues), shaking the walls. No through-breeze flowed thanks to the architecturally flawed placement of the windows. When Chris and Maggie moved to Brisbane for some unfathomable reason, Stanton stopped.

Bob and I went onto HC. Simon started releasing solo records under the Fupper name. Simon and I also had another band called Blackhorse. We released a ten-inch called *Rides* and played a few shows. The keen ear could spot a future HC bass line or two on the *Rides* record.

Stanton had had a good run, though. We were decent for around eight months of our nine-year history, which is as good as most bands achieve. Search your soul, your favourite band dropped the ball years ago. Anyhow. We started our own label –

we called it Jonson Family – and released our records and records by other bands.

Although we were influenced by all the big keepers of the DIY music torch, the main reason we started doing the label with any level of *oomph* was this:

After three or four years of not much we decided to record four songs in New Cross, South London. We released it as a seven-inch called the *Four Walls Ep*. It cost £546.38 (I still have the invoice) for 545 records. We wanted 500. Pressing plants always over-press, then charge you for it. Clever. Butchers do the same with meat. Dairy shops do the same with cheese. We hand stamped them all in our living room in Wood Green, North London. Then we had a pile of 545 records to get rid of. Over the next few months we sent them places and sold them at shows and swapped with people and all sorts. Rough Trade took a good amount and even ordered more. They took 40 in the end which was incredible. Just as the trickle of sales was turning into a standstill of sales, a proper record label became interested. They were called Che Records and they were guilty of releasing records by the band Urusei Yatsura, who we'd heard of and some other bands that I can't remember the names of now and hadn't heard of then.

We had some meetings with them, they saw us play a number of times and we sucked up to them and got stressed if they didn't call for a day. This went on. We then got put into a studio and recorded the worst sounding four songs ever. Very soon after that it was all over. Our dream of supporting Urusei Yatsura at The Astoria was up in flames. Our hopes of someone paying for everything were down the toilet. We'd spent a year hanging on their every word, thinking all they were saying was gospel, and when it came to it we massively screwed up in the studio. The engineer was terrible.

The studio was terrible. The atmosphere was terrible. We didn't have enough time. All these are excuses we probably used but, ultimately, we'd messed up through lack of preparation and having no confidence in the studio. We couldn't explain what we wanted.

A lot was learned from this debacle.

From this point on, with Stanton and then on into Hey Colossus, we've waited for no one in terms of releasing records. Leave a bloody trail, strew the carcasses throughout your music life. Drop records in all shapes and sizes from as many angles and distances as you can. Play all you can. Do all you can. I swear, dealing with this proper label opened our eyes to the way one should conduct one's self. Do it with absolute confidence, that even if you're going wrong at least it's your wrong. You own it.

A quote from Nas, creator of one of the greatest rap albums of all time, *Illmatic:*

> "I never understand people who don't work on their art, people who work on their ego and want to seek praise but haven't got anywhere yet."
>
> – from *Rapture,* the Netflix documentary series

This, for me, is the current state of the social media whirl. Hunting out praise for a first rehearsal photo, searching for an ego boost instead of working on your thing. Whatever your thing is. We may never get anywhere doing this but as this tale goes on it'll become apparent that playing live and travelling and meeting people is our way of spreading the word. Travelling to learn from others. The failure of Stanton to sort out this label deal taught us this. Not every band is destined to be enormous but every band has the capability to please the band members. It was time to work on this, and not work on the ego.

At the beginning, HC was a five-piece and we formed through knowing each other and finding James Parker on the Fracture Forum – back when forums were a thing. *Fracture* was a UK-based punk rock fanzine, our country's answer to *Maximum Rocknroll* (long-running US monthly punk rock bible, now RIP) I suppose. It was decent. I heard it got run into the ground when certain labels didn't pay for advertising. Who knows. Print media eh? Our posting read: "Forming band. Can meets Fudge Tunnel, get in touch." Bob and I wanted to do a heftier thing. Ian Scanlon was in a band called Econoline who released records and did tours. James Parker was in a band called Yeast who released records and did tours and Tim Hall hadn't drummed for 10 years (his last drumming job had been with the Brighton band, I'm Being Good) but I worked with him, so he had to say yes. All fancied it. Our first rehearsal was in Stoke Newington, the Walthamstow of 2003, a trendy place where everyone wanted to live. None of us lived there but the name of the studio, Zen Arcade, named after the Hüsker Dü album, was reason enough to go there.

We kept a diary of the shows we played, back when people looked at websites, back when Facebook didn't exist, before even Myspace. Here's Ian on the first show:

> This was a good start, despite me having to walk all the way to Stockwell tube station (15 minutes) carrying my amp (which was pretty heavy). I don't think we hung around for Thread. me and James went home and got really drunk with Marianne and my old house mate Nick which was ruling. I had such a bad hangover the next day that I didn't get out of bed until 4pm.

The first song we wrote was called 'A Witch is Born'. I say we wrote it, in fact Ian brought the idea in saying that someone else had written it. Mr Chris Summerlin, who will doubtless crop up later, was the riff-master on this occasion. Him and Ian were thinking of doing a band called Oklahomo and they had one riff. We stole it and they never happened. A shame, as the band name would have been worth the entry fee alone.

Over the first three months we rehearsed and wrote five songs and learned a cover. At our first show at the aforementioned Buffalo Bar we played all six songs. We did the same set over the next few.

Thursday October 2nd, 2003. The Swan, Tottenham, with Majority Rule and Amongst The Missing (due to being stuck in Spain, Majority Rule were replaced by Sin 'O The East)

Tim Hall:

The mighty Swan. Can't remember anything about the other bands but I do remember we went off like a bomb and being painfully unfit I nearly collapsed at the end of the show due to exhaustion.

Sunday October 26th, 2003. Upstairs at The Garage, with Red Ashes (formerly Yeast), Woe and Birdhouse Project

Ian:

This was a bit poor as I recall although the music between bands was good and I had chilli and chips from the Wetherspoons around the corner.

James:

Bit difficult for me to be too emo about Red Ashes finishing [Red Ashes was James' other band], as for one that had really run its course, and for two, I was happy as Larry doing this Hey Colossus thing that had somehow transpired.

Saturday November 15th, 2003. Vintners Parrot, Worthing, with The Lords, The Burning Hull, Yenpox and Semioneside

If I remember rightly Brentford won two-one, pulling it back in the last few minutes, I almost punched a hole in the roof of my car celebrating on whatever road it is you take from London to Worthing.

Tim:

Brilliant night. My Mum and Dad (who are in their late 60s/ early 70s) came to see me play. They wore earplugs. Total respect to them for coming. Ian was very, very, very drunk for this gig. Him and Dave Croft spent most of the afternoon in the pub. Coming from Littlehampton down the coast I used to play shows at this place when it was called the Thieves Kitchen back in the late 1980s early 1990s. Lords totally slayed. Local bands seemed to have the hump that 'out of towners' were playing – go figure. Colin from Edgeworld put the show on. Top gent that he is!

Sunday November 16th, 2003. 201 Coldharbour Lane, Brixton, with Cat On Form, Birds Of Paradise, The Lords and Claque

COF were really good, BOP had Saxon haircuts and pulled some nice poses, The Lords were naturally brilliant, and Claque were also real good playing bass/violin, and drums. We've played worse proper venues in comparison to this squat.

And then into December. We thought it'd be a great idea to record all the songs we knew and release it on Jonson Family. So over one weekend we played this show on the Friday:

Friday December 5th, 2003. Upstairs at The Garage, Highbury, with Black Eyes and Bullet Union

Tim:

Probably the best gig we had played to date. An incredible night. Black Eyes had so much equipment that they couldn't fit on the stage. The place was RAMMED with loads of people left outside. Part of the very fine Silver Rocket club night. Southern Records checked us out. Harry Harris and John Loder stood by the side of the stage throughout our set. They are in a bunch of photos somewhere. They never contacted us afterwards. Black Eyes were excellent.

Then on the Saturday and Sunday we snuck into Bob's work and got a friend – Phil Rodgers from Northampton who went under the name Place Position – to bring his portable studio and we recorded all six songs we knew. Five of which were to make up the debut record and the cover, 'Money', by Fang, to go on a split seven-inch with Lords. We decided we wanted 'A Witch Is Born' on one side of the record on its own. We found out that the optimum time to quality ratio for an LP is 18 minutes, so we set up a clock and made sure the tune was exactly 18 minutes long. Drones and jamming to book-end the main tune. At the time bands like Sunn0))) were beginning to make waves and they were masters of the drone, so we gave it a go. Thing is, they use vast amps made of rocks and boulders and hellfire and have recording studios cut from the surface of Mars. We had Carlsbro Stingray combo amps directly from the 1980s. Bass cabs with only three speakers working. Guitars that cost almost £100 and our pal Phil's portable studio. But, hey. No one was listening, so it didn't matter.

We mixed and mastered the record over the week. Then sent

it off to be pressed up. One week later, on December 19th, two weeks after recording it, we got 500 copies of our debut record, *Hates You and You and You*, back on heavy black vinyl in a gatefold sleeve. It was that quick. Have a look at people complaining nowadays about record pressing times; it can be up to three months or more. No one was pressing vinyl in the early 2000s. It was a dead format. Being total nerds for it though, we ploughed on through. Consequently, around this time all the pressing plants closed, digital music grew large and CDs began dying. Vinyl has come back now (it's a fashion thing but I don't care, I can now buy Adele on double LP in Sainsburys) and there's nowhere to make them apart from one place in the Czech Republic. Fair play to them. If you win when backing a horse fit for glue you deserve all the gold in the hills. Stick with what you believe in, it'll come back round. As Lemmy said, back when he wasn't as dead: 'Stick around long enough and they'll call you a legend', and he said that to Mudhoney who could just as easily have said it, as could ten or twenty or thirty other bands. Even sticking it out for ten years at Royal Mail gets you a pin badge. I'm almost there. The sky will be dark with hats.

In the late 1990s a new radio station was set up in London called Resonance FM. It properly started airing in 2002. It was based on Denmark Street, 'Tin Pan Alley', where all the music shops are too expensive and the rubbish fills the roads and the only reason you'd go down there, musician or not, was to get to The Angel. When pints were becoming expensive, The Angel at the end of Denmark Street was an oasis in the London booze desert. A Sam Smith's pub, the prices were set at £1.87 or £2.01 in an attempt to stop the bar staff from stealing as they had to open the till to sort change for the poor traveller. Nice faith shown in your staff there, Mr Smith. It was an old school pub with windows you couldn't see in and day-time miseries slumped over tables. A totally beautiful scene in a fast and forward moving international city, a scene direct from Dickens or Withnail and I. The flats opposite still had the bomb curtains hanging in the windows or so I was told by one slumped hero. No idea if it was true but those flats are long gone now and have been replaced by a modern lump that reeks of shiny shoes and no socks. I have a problem with 'no socks' or 'trainer socks' or whatever. If you get a chance have a look at Barney from Napalm Death playing Glastonbury back in 2017, *that's* how to wear socks: up to the knees and be proud.

It was a relief Resonance FM was set up. XFM was in its death throes, choking on playlist hell and corporate balderdash. It had just been bought by Capital and was almost instantly destroyed. Elisa, my now wife but then partner, and I used to fax (yes, fax) XFM and ask for lesser known Dischord bands such as Smart Went Crazy at 2am and within minutes John Kennedy would be playing them. I wonder whether that was the only time Smart Went Crazy got played on UK radio. You should definitely check out Smart Went Crazy. They did two records, both with a particularly quirky take on the 1990s DC punk shtick. The singer, Chad Clark, took them above and beyond. XFM is still going as RadioX or something which sounds like a particularly gnarly late-night babe station sort of affair. I don't know. People cannot stop messing with things. Sometimes when it's happening and happening well I wonder if the people at the top cannot fathom it and analyze it and probe it like a MK Ultra operator, zapping it to death to try and work out what is making it good.

I once listened to an hour-long show on Resonance where they'd edited together the gaps and pauses between the words said by journalists during the Gulf War. And I enjoyed it. They gave us our first ever airplay and session. We played three tunes from our first record and I gave an interview which, when I listened back, I was shocked at my slack-jawed, thundering, consonant-dropping non-accent. We've since played a couple more sessions. The station is now based south of the river, near Borough Market and it's still totally vital listening. Within 24-hours of playing on the station for the first time, Tim Cedar from Part Chimp rang and said he'd dug it. This meant a lot to us. We'd been watching him whack and hack in a fair few joyful bands through the years. Drumming in The Love Blobs, drumming in Penthouse, manipulating six strings and bellowing in Ligament (supported by Mogwai [!] upstairs at The Garage, most memorably), and now doing the same in Part Chimp, who destroy all bands. He rang, and it was good.

After our first show and based on a live review from Drowned In Sound, naturally our first ever piece of press (Mr Mike Diver, take a bow, for you wrote it. I always remember the first time), EMI e-mailed. Yes, EMI. We ignored it but had a day chuckling about it. We were already ancient. If they could have seen us puffing and wheezing during load-in at The Buffalo Bar they would not only not have e-mailed us they would have asked all venues in the UK to install defibrillators at the top and bottom of all staircases as standard. These aged fools are gonna do themselves some damage. EMI fell apart in 2012, still reeling from our lack of reply.

The first day of five European shows, May 2018, four of which will be with Sumac. Aaron Turner from the band has been in touch for ten years now. We've been swapping records and chatting. This is the second time he's asked us to tour with them. We couldn't do it the first time as Paul was on his honeymoon. Priorities. Among many other strings to his bow, Aaron was in the band Isis, is in Old Man Gloom, runs Sige Records and is part of the Hydrahead Records organisation. We're excited to be hanging out for a few days.

The last month has been like having two full-time jobs. My manager at work asked me three weeks ago if I was all right. I was probably looking frazzled. Both Hey Colossus and Henry Blacker have been busy, playing live and recording. Work has carried on, five days a week, 6am starts. It's been the same for Roo – two bands, a family and a full-time job. We knew March through to May was going to be brutal. We can now see the light. These five shows are the end of the busy time and we're going to head into summer with only three shows booked. We want to get on with our twelfth album.

Up at 3am, Roo, myself and Elisa drive to Bristol to pick up Will. We meet Rhys, Bob and Paul in Caterham at 7.30 and head to Dover. Our boat is sailing at 10.15. It's Bank Holiday weekend so the port is busy. The lorries are gridlocked back up the A20 for five miles. We file past them and join the school coaches and families all queuing to get onto whichever boat heading to whichever destination. Today, passport control don't care. Everyone is being waved onwards. Sometimes it can take forever but today the person in the booth is being paid to shrug and get everyone through as quickly as possible. We're ninety minutes early for our sailing. By the time we get through the ticket checks and passport control we end up driving straight on to the boat.

We're in a hire van that I picked up on Thursday. It crashed it down with rain and water poured into the rear seating area. 'It's a van, what do you expect' was the answer from the hire company. I had to go to the local tyre replacement company on the Friday after work to fix a puncture, then hit the supermarket to stock the house up for Stan and Freddie while we're gone. Lay down some ground rules: if you burn the house down please save my 100 favourite records. Leave those early Radiohead twelve-inch's behind. I don't care if they're worth money, I'm still ashamed to own them. Those records you buy when you're an impressionable youngster, when you've been hoodwinked by the press, they haunt you forever. I even bought a Shed Seven record once. The review made them sound so exciting. The record made them sound so unexciting. On this level I'm jealous of the young, being able to listen to the music before buying. How many records have I bought on a whim that haven't been good enough? How many have I got hold of that I've persisted with and are now my very favourite records? I reckon you've got to take the massive defeats to make the victories so much sweeter.

The van is fine, it drives well. The weather is looking good, so leaking won't happen. I am writing this at 9.23 on the morning after the first show. Today I am an optimist. Last night's show in Nijmegen at Doornroosje was Will's first show. It was in a venue in the centre of town, next to the train station. It's a purpose-built space; parking in the building, a huge backstage area that deals with the two venues inside. The room we're playing in holds 600 people. The other room is the big room. Nick Mulvey is playing next door. His dressing room is next to ours, which we are sharing with Sumac. All the bands playing both rooms eat dinner at the same time. The food is arguably the best food we've ever had at a show. I overheard the members of the other bands saying the same thing. Joe Preston is playing bass with Sumac on this tour. We all know him from the Melvins. He briefly wore a bandana at the end of the night and was ramming the leftover backstage food into a bag to take away. The food was that good. We all put bandanas on and started ramming leftovers into bags. The show was splendid. Will played perfectly. 'Honest to God', 'Back in the Room', 'Oktave Dokkter', 'Sisters and Brothers', 'Black and Gold', 'Pope Long Haul', 'March of the Headaches', 'Dead Eyes'. Fourty-one minutes. We overran by one minute. Sumac were crushing.

RED GIANT

from II

2004

Back in the Walthamstow days, once upon a time, we got some new neighbours. Well, they were next door-but-one neighbours. Sheila and Ray Levitt lived directly next door. Sheila and Ray were somewhere around fifty-five years old. You could tell the time of day by when Sheila did the vacuuming. They said: 'What's the point of getting a new kitchen NOW?', even though Sheila's parents were still alive and longevity was rife in the family. They were those sort of folk. Frozen roast potato people. Genuinely lovely couple. We would pass our boys over the fence to them. They so wanted grandchildren (which they eventually got). Old school, East London. Next to them a family moved in. They had children the same age as ours, so our kids played in the street and gardens together. The first time we went to their house, to collect an errant offspring, I walked through the front room into the room in the middle of the house and it was full of brand new amps and band gear. I said: "This room is full of amps and band gear."

Julie Sims, for that was her name, said: "Yes, I was once in a band and we got signed and we released an album. Then we recorded another album and the label didn't like it so instead of releasing it they dropped us and wiped the debt so now this room is full of amps and band gear".

I said: "Oh".

The band was Tiger. For those who were monitoring the *NME* and *Sounds* and *Melody Maker* in the 1990s bands like this came and went so damn quick. I didn't hear them until after meeting Julie around 2003 time. So, they came, blew up for thirty seconds, and shrivelled down again long before I saw their album for a pound in the local Oxfam and bought it out of loyalty/intrigue. I do remember all their press though. They seemed to get signed and given vast sums of cash for having mullets and having the stones to play Indie rock music with ape drapes instead of bowl cuts. The money that was pouring around the music industry from the 1980s up until the early 2000s was sort of disgusting. The way it would get lucky with a band, Nirvana, for example, and then spend the following three years signing every band from Seattle. Along with every band from the Western world who sang while sucking their lower lip in (the 'yarl' – as coined by King Buzzo of the band Melvins, a band who will outlive the pyramids) and wearing distressed clothing. It really summed up the lack of imagination within the industry.

Tiger's first record probably did okay. They were everywhere in the press and on stages. The second record was recorded, at some cost, but instead of releasing it the label cut its losses and dropped the band. Reasoning that the cost of promotion, distribution and press and radio was too much, and no money was going to be made. Tiger's moment had passed. Their second record lost in the machinations of 'the industry', a decision taken somewhere to piss in the gas tank of the band, stuttering it to a standstill.

Their debut is decent, a sort of cross between Stereolab and The Buzzcocks. Look up 'Shining in the Wood' on YouTube. Maybe the second record would have blown up like *Nevermind* or *Appetite for Destruction* or *Rumours* or maybe it would have sunk like they were predicting. But you'd think if the people making the decisions had taken a week off the nose candy, the cost of releasing it would have been covered and they would have found out one way or the other.

It's almost like the internet needed to come along and wipe all the dinosaurs out, hurl a firework into the room and cause panic. The irony being most people who claim to be DIY music lovers would probably have a fifty-fifty split between independent releases and major label releases in their top twenty. Some ZZ Top, a slice of Captain Beefheart, a Kendrick Lamar record or maybe some Stevie Wonder. They all sound incredible. They've all been through the machine, been washed and spruced up and marketed to the end of time. They're all makers of incredible records. What can you say? A shake up was needed. The www came along and did the shaking. Time to move on. Time to change the way things happen.

But still, back in the early 2000s we ran our record label because despite all I said before I love the workings of the music industry. I love its flaws and the fallen bands, and I love it when there's a freak success. I follow the paths of massive stars like Ed Sheeran; how they've been marketed and sold is fascinating. I love the joyful, unpredicted leaps through the ranks like the Fat White Family, Goat, Richard Dawson or Sleaford Mods. Over the last few years I'd been writing a blog that no one read purely to 'get it down before my mind was too fried'. It was called *Memories of Running a Shitty Record Label* (*MORASRL*) and here are some 'highlights' from it:

Look back through your record collection. When did web addresses start replacing actual number, road, town, city, postcode ridden addresses? It's quite a fun thing to do if you're a 'sleeve starer' like myself. In fact, I can stare at a sleeve, the front and back, for the whole duration of a side of vinyl. 20 minutes. Easy.

Our first record had 22 Palmerston Rd, Wood Green, N22 as the label contact. For around six months we got no mail. Then after that we still got no mail. We didn't get any mail ever. Our postman had an easy life. Even back then, people had stopped writing letters, awaiting the arrival of email. Email will save us! They would have cried had they known what they were awaiting.

We sent a copy of the seven-inch to John Peel. We managed to find his home address rather than sending it to the BBC. We were a team of Columbos.

John Peel played it.

Rough Trade then sold a load.

Then Cargo (a record distributor) took 100. Having a distributor nowadays is possibly not the way to go for a small and new record label. Mail order is big business and gets you more cash. Everyone orders piles of toss from the www, and this would be money for you unfiltered by the grabbing claws of a distributor. As mentioned, the www didn't really exist in 1998 so we were pretty pleased with ourselves. We patted ourselves on the back. We thought we were the dog's danglers.

Peel. There's nowt like him now. The BBC had no respect for him when he was alive, burying him later and later in the schedules. It wasn't till he died did they reluctantly act like they gave a monkeys.

....that's enough, we'll come back to this.

It's now 2005 and time for HC to record a new record. We called it *II*. Zeppelin did it so why not us?

To rub salt into the wound of our standing in the world, and to utterly prove the difference between a massive major label band and a 'teetering-on-the-edge,-selling-500-LPs' band, we were playing shows like this:

Friday January 23rd, 2005. Margate Lido, with Blind Jackson
Blind Jackson sounded like Reef. They probably thought we sounded like The Deftones.

Tim:
One of the strangest shows we've ever played at what can only be described as a fading seafront Kontiki bar. The crowd was a mix of scantily clad teenage Goth girls and pubescent 15-year-old Goth boys. I think we totally confused them all, but they seemed to like Drug Widow or at least the nodding head bit. Split before Blind Jackson to get the train home, but they sounded a bit like Toploader, I think. We all felt like dirty old men at this show.

Ian:
Margate, the stuff that dreams are made of. Mind you, me and Tim got dead scared that we were going to get offed on the train back through Kent. I reckon if we did it again now it'd be happy slap central.

James:
Oh dear, mind you was very funny watching the kids work out there was a 'mosh part' in Red Nails, and doing some formation headbanging. We are doing this for the kids.

To really mark out the difference between the 'haves' and the 'we don't care if we have its' we managed to sneak into AC/DC's studio near Angel tube in London. It was called Albert's. We set up in the middle of the enormous live room and recorded our next album. Drummer Tim had a contact who could get us the key, so we got in on a Saturday morning with Phil (he who recorded our first record at Bob's workplace) and all his recording gear and we recorded six tunes and went home Sunday evening.

We had to go back again the following weekend and do it all again as Phil accidentally scrubbed all the first recordings.

I can't begin to tell you how overjoyed we were.

'Red Giant' is a long song, eight or nine minutes. There's no way I'm going to listen to it and time it accurately for you, I have things to do. It has one chord in it for the most part and then a hang note every few minutes. Half way through it changes from being loud and heavy to loud and slightly not as heavy. The main note is 'G', feel free to play along. If you happen to be a guitar nerd (I am not, but I have many trusted friends who are obsessed with Japanese guitars or Rickenbackers or whatever else. I ask them advice and their words pour into one ear, dance around what's left of my brain, take a dump on my mind, and pour out the other leaving me none the wiser) then this will be fascinating for you: James had a posh guitar at the time, a PRS I believe, and he tuned the fat string down to G, so he could play it open. It sounded very low and floppy. If he played it gently for the duration it almost stayed in tune for the full length of the song. In fairness it did add some chunk to the whole affair while Bob and Ian wailed away and Tim and I plodded through, counting the loops until each tiny change, giving each other a nod and switching. We played this song, and its seemingly simplistic song structure, a lot. People seemed to like it. Well, the sort of people that came to see us anyway.

Back around the early 2000s there was a band called Isis, which at the time meant something somewhat different to what it does now. You're a brave person if you're still wearing the T-Shirts. Wasn't there a dog in a soap opera who had the name Isis who had to be killed off? How many dogs in TV shows get killed off? Anyhow, 'Red Giant' was a bit of an Isis rip off. Sorry Aaron, we meant it out of respect. Isis were part of the Hydrahead Records stable, which was run in an inspirational way. From the art to the sound they had it down. I saw the band once at an ATP festival at Camber Sands and they were so loud the power kept cutting off and all the lights came on.

I still like the tune. Ian and James' vocals on it are perfectly desperate. The mix is as good as we could have got considering the whole record was recorded (twice) in 48 hours. This included setting up a whole studio and all our gear. And, of course, sneaking about AC/DC's studio while a proper big band was in the rehearsal area looking at us like we were in the wrong. I heard their music; it was certainly them in the wrong.

We released the CD of it on Jonson Family for Europe and Shifty Records released it in America. Wakusei Records released it on sweet red vinyl.

Around this time nothing made me happier than seeing records being split-released by multi labels. Underground doom bands or extreme speed twenty-second-long punx were putting records out, limited to 300, with ten label names on the back. Each label ponied up for ten per cent of the press, getting thirty each to sell online, dotted around the world. It was a no-brainer. It was clever. It was, though, a total and utter ball ache to organise.

In fact, here from the *MORASRL* Blog, I knocked up this post in regards a record we helped release by our good friends

Trencher, them of the Casio Keyboard from HC's first ever show:

Something that seemed to happen a lot in the late '90s and early 2000s or I only noticed it then (it could have been going on for years) was the 'multi-label release'. It was a genius idea: tiny band releases record on numerous tiny labels dotted around the planet, thereby spreading the slop in one giant sweep. It saved the hassle of one tiny label doing all the leg work. It also looked ridiculous / amusing when all the labels logos were laid out on the rear of the album.

Trencher were big fans of this malarkey. So, when it came to releasing their seminal work, *When Dracula Thinks: "Look At Me",* they knew what they wanted.

The situation was confused by the fact they'd had the recording of the album financed by a company called 'Punish Productions' who were hunting out a record deal for them. When Geffen didn't come knocking they started slumming it and asked us, along with piles of other shitty record labels. We jumped at the chance. We had to pay to get the recordings. We had never paid for recordings before and never did again. The cost was spread over the six labels involved. We owned the recordings. Like what a proper label does. We puffed on our massive fat cigars and stroked ourselves, satisfied. We laughed a maniacal laugh. We released the Trencher album on CD.

The labels involved, and their different catalogue numbers: Victory Garden Records – VG22, Jonson Family – JFR 012, SuperFi Records – SF010, A Tree In A Field Records – TREE006, Action Index Records – AIR03, La Vida No Es Un Mus – NOMUS001

The CDs sold well, but we only had about 100 of them due to them being split left and right between the band and label and distribution. I doubt we broke even on it. Another success.

Trencher then signed to Southern, who released their follow up record, *Lips*. Southern then re-issued the album that all us shitty labels had put out and owned the rights to. We're still waiting for the cheque.

Yes, the album got re-released three years later. We couldn't say no to the band even though we had the rights to the music. They were friends and we didn't want to halt their obvious march to the top. Not entirely sure they made it to the top. I don't rightly recall.

But, anyhow, for HC's second record we had two labels doing the CD and a third doing the vinyl. It was a decent way to get the music out there, budget style, DIY style. If you can't fight the fight with vast sums of cash, fight it with word of mouth.

Once we'd played some shows for this record and done our bit to promote it, and disappointed some people:

Wednesday August 25th, 2005. 93 Feet East, London, with The Murder Of Rosa Luxemburg
I think we played four long hellish songs and bored people to death.

Ian:
Yeah, we only did four songs and the kid who put it on kind of whined that we didn't play 'the fast stuff'. We're not a juke box, mate. Particularly true as he didn't put any money in us.

And upset some people:

Friday October 22nd, 2005. The Star, Guildford, with Todd
  Tim:

Ha ha – soundman trouble. Todd were good as you'd expect. Local Soundgimp got the *real* hump with us at this gig. Some jumped up local twenty-one-year-old flick-fringed prick who didn't want us to check our gear before we went on. Then told us the *minute* we finished that we played loud to cover up the fact that our songs were shit and we couldn't play our instruments. He was lucky he didn't get a slap. Guildford on a Friday night. Wannabe 15-year-old chavs getting arrested for underage drinking in darkly lit shopping precincts. Horrible. Still fun though! Got train home and got stuck at Clapham Junction for an hour. Bummer.

And made friends with some police:

Sunday August 8th, 2005. Squat show off Oxford Street, with Fucking Big Monster, Jets Vs Sharks and Chillerton
  Ian:

The other squat shows I did for these kids were better organised than this one and in slightly more accessible places (this was just by Selfridges, so tough to drive to), but the sound at this one was great, and the vibe was good. Despite having to load gear up *loads* of stairs. Also, I think Bob blew his amp again at this show and plugged into Joe's amp to keep on rocking. I remember we did Red Giant and the kids seem to dig it. I totally screamed my head off and that seemed to keep them interested. The rozzers came but I was down the road buying water as this place *was hot* and they obviously had to keep the windows shut. We played in what was probably some kind of meeting room or board room as the place was an abandoned office. The police were cool, and I think the whole bill got to play so all in all a sweet day.

James:

This was unbelievably hot, sweating before we started, and we began with Red Giant which just caved the place in. Probably the loudest we've ever been, certainly in gigs without big PAs. Rest of gig equally raging, then afterwards I was sitting outside, and the police turned up saying there have been several complaints about the noise. I chatted to them amiably and failed to completely own up it was our fault ha-ha.

I thoroughly enjoyed this. It was, as Ian and James say, *hot.* I really enjoyed Jets V Sharks. It was dark and busy, and they were good.

And played with a band who were soon to become famous who we clearly didn't dig much:

Saturday August 7th, 2005. The Freebutt, Brighton, with Hot Chip

Tim:

Another Freebutt show. Bit quiet as so much was going on in Brighton that night. Nothing blew up though and we played as a five-piece this time. It was Gay Pride in Brighton so whole town was packed. Trencher were playing at pub across road, so after we played everyone bundled over to see them. Hot Chip were a Bronski Beat-like synth band. Pretty crappy.

The next gig brought another band who were on their way to being big news, along with another soundman issue – I have since heard the soundman got locked in the toilet by Comets this night, they were so pissed off with him:

Tuesday January 18th, 2006. Hobgoblin, Brighton, with Comets On Fire

A photographer from one of those Brighton mags spent the whole of COF's gig dancing in front of them like a pole dancer trying to get the right rocking shot.

Tim:

Originally this gig was supposed to be at the Freebutt but due to a booking issue (not Phil the promoters fault) had to be moved to the incredibly small upstairs room at the Hobgoblin. We arrived at the venue to find the band being harangued by idiotic pony-tailed metalhead sound prick who was making COF turn down to ridiculously quiet levels. There are great features on this night in recent editions of *Comes With a Smile* and *Loose Lips* magazines. We played and just turned it up – sending soundcock into a lather. COF rocked it as you would expect. Place held about 70 people. More crammed in than that, with loads of folks locked out.

Ian:

Comets On Fire ruled and so did the bloke who stood in front of me smiling for the whole set (though I think he may have been on drugs). Grubbs burger gratefully consumed here.

After a good number of shows like this we released our second split seven-inch single. The first was being the aforementioned Lords split with the tune 'Money' that we recorded at the first session. This time it was the song 'Ghost Ship' that we put on our side of the record with the excellently named band, The Phil Collins Three.

5

GHOST SHIP
from split seven-inch with Phil Collins Three
2005

This tune was recorded at the same time as *II*, which, if you've totally forgotten, was our second record. You think it's confusing now, just hold onto yourself. It was released by Victory Garden Records, 300 copies pressed. A split single with the just-now-mentioned Phil Collins Three who were from 'London-on-Sea', Brighton. Then, about 10 years later, in 2015, the label sent us about 200 copies of the same record but miss-pressed by the pressing plant, where our tune is on the PC3 side and vice versa. The pressing plant screwed up and had to redo it back in 2005, telling Victory Garden they could keep the 300 blunders. They were under the bed apparently, for over a decade. This is exactly where all unsold records go. Or, if you're lucky enough to have a garage, they can sit in there forever. You don't need to feed them, they will just sit there. Every time you go out to get your trowel or camping stuff or whatever, they will look at you and shrug, 'We did our bit, your songs suck'. You will think about getting the band back together. You will not get the band back together. You will think about throwing them away. You will not throw them away. You will think about setting up a little online shop to sell them to the baying masses. You will not do this either. We gave the miss-pressed records away free with mail-order to people who had no idea about the existence of the record and were even more baffled by the totally different sounding sides and the fact the PC3 side should have had three tunes while ours only had one, yet the labels said different. Best to leave people in the dark. I doubt they got played.

The seven-inch format, despite vinyl's supposed rise in popularity, is priced so appallingly that it's essentially taking itself down to Beachy Head and jumping to the rocks below. You can pay up to £10 for a new seven-inch now. If you're the sort of person who is buying new seven-inch's for £10 I'd put money on you also having a guitar on your wall and a drawer full of trainer socks.

Both this song and *II* were recorded on September 11, 2004. The artwork had a crashing plane on the rear. Very tasteful. Sorry, years on.

It's a sort of doomy bluesy sea shanty. I hear the band Come in there. They had a splendid record called *Eleven: Eleven*. Thalia Zedek's vocals were the winner, really marvellous. Not that we talked about it, but there's certainly something similar going on. Ian and Bob did a dual vocal thing where Ian did the verses and Bob tucked in on the chorus like he was tucking into a particularly raw steak. Ian was eating a bean stew. It was the contrast that did it for me. Vyvyan versus Neil the hippy.

We did two launch shows for this record, one in 'London on Sea', Brighton, and one in Real-London.

Tuesday December 9th, 2005. The Freebutt, Brighton, with Phil Collins Three and Giddy Motors

Tim:

I remember more about Phil Collins Three's costumes than anything else about this gig. Dressed as missiles I think. Giddy

Motors I missed as I was upstairs having a drink. We seemed to play the Freebutt a lot last year. Always friendly and a good place to play.

Ian:

Grubbs burgers makes money out of bands. Sweet. I went home after Phil Collins Three, Christ it was a Tuesday night.

Tuesday January 25th, 2006. Infinity Club, Mayfair, London, with Phil Collins Three

Once we finished playing there was an audible sigh of relief around the place.

Tim:

The Infinity seemed to be full of art students waiting for us to finish so they could get off with each other. Had a kind of 1980s cocaine vibe to the place.

Ian:

We played well but again the blank looks on the teenage faces were somewhat off-putting. I think they expected one of us to die on stage or something. A review of this said we were a "Math rock band." That person is dead now

That second show didn't sound too good. Who puts rock gigs on in Mayfair? It's just asking for trouble. Also, around this point, once we'd put up around 40 or 50 show reviews on the www site people started reading them. They got some traction. Well, they did from some quarters as each time we had a pop at a band or a venue or a soundman they would end up reading it and it would get back to us. After one particularly gruelling night in North London one of us commented on the other bands being less than good and consequently we never got to play Derby as the affronted band seemingly ran the town. Also note how Bob very rarely writes anything for these. I need to ask him about this.

With the 'Ghost Ship' seven-inch, and *II,* that came out around the same time we got enough press and interest to somehow land a Radio One session. It was for Huw Stephens who is still on the radio now and, as with all good Radio One DJs, has a double life where they do the BBC's work on the one hand, covering daytime shows, presenting sordid awards to unworthy winners, all of that. Yet, in the evening, he has a show where he'll play stuff he likes. The pay off. Like when feeding your child, 'You can have pudding, but you have to eat this plate of cauliflower first'. But I wonder, is the BBC a strict parent? If your child says no to the cauliflower will you buckle and give the cake anyway? They've got to eat something, right? You can't let them die. Bad parents give pudding when the cauliflower isn't eaten. Terrible parents starve their children to prove a point.

We'd had some history with Radio One before. John Peel had played a song from the first record. 'Sounds a bit like Pink Floyd,' were his words. Of course, back in 2004 and for thirty-seven years before, this was a basic ambition for all bands – a Peel play was something to tell your parents. But, late on in 2004 he was gone, and the BBC made a right old scene of it. They'd buried him in the schedules. Later and later. Hoping he'd go quietly yet he showed up and played what he wanted to play, and he kept on. A lot of the good folk in music get more celebrated when they're gone, than when they're around. They get taken for granted or people are just bored and want the new thing. Then Prince dies or Bowie dies or Mark E Smith dies and out of the woodwork come all the vampires. A feeding frenzy to get the column inches, to get the soundbite. I think my point is that the BBC is a terrible parent.

To prove how excellent Peel was, the previous few years he had played around thirty Jonson Family related songs, maybe more. We'd come up trumps with a couple of compilations we released, the *Twominutemen* double seven-inch. We put 16 bands on each compilation, four songs a side, no song over two minutes. So, there were thirty-two songs spread over two compilations released a year apart, 2002 and 2003. It was the sort of thing a man like Peel could totally get his teeth into, helped somewhat by the song brevity guidelines we'd employed. He then got us into Maida Vale, picking five bands from the first compilation and giving them ten minutes each to play live on his show. The Tenminutemen nights. On my death bed, if asked, these nights will be on my list of 'shit, that was decent' in my life.

On the *MORASRL* blog the first session went along these lines:

Through the year of our lord 2002 John Peel would go on to play every tune from the twominutemen compilation on his radio programme, all sixteen of 'em. On one show he played a tune from the Stanton album AND a tune from the compilation, two JF tunes in one show. Through the year of our lord 2002 we were like pigs in shitty shit. We thunked we was unfuckwithable. Of course, none of this crud lasted, we wasn't brunged up to believe in obtaining too much success. But the year of our lord 2002 was a major blip in a life thus far spent charging toward our collective ultimate aims of drunken destitution.

While working at SRD I made good friends with a Canadian character by the name of Marc Brown. He was a go-getter. He would stomp around the warehouse, head buried in his shoulders, demanding his life be better. He had seen success in the music industry back in Canada and wanted to achieve the same in the UK. He left SRD to work at Creation Records, home to lots of mouth and no trousers bands, probably garnering bucketloads more stories than I'm making up in this tale of japery and knee tremblers. Once Creation folded in a cloud of powder he set up his own radio plugging outfit.

A radio plugger is someone a big record label pays quids too in the hope of getting played on the radio. The radio plugger has the contacts to make it happen. And with fingers crossed and cocks crossed, and tits crossed it may just happen, and the new James Blunt will be discovered, and everyone will go home happy.

Anyhow, I bring Mr. Marc Brown into the tale because he was to provide an integral cog in the folly that was to follow.

Bob had been dealing with trying to get radio plays for JF releases. He would pop CDRs and records into radio people's hands. Bob worked in central London. Radio is based in central London. Must have the best signal there.

Through a combination of Marc and myself being drunk in the Queens Head, Turnpike Lane and discussing stuff, and Bob, and Louise Kattenhorn (Peel's producer), an idea was somehow concocted. The Tenminutemen. A night where five bands from the comp were to play, live at Maida Vale, on Peel's show, ten minutes each. Although we vaguely knew Louise, it was Marc who gave it a professional push, he probably had a BlackBerry by this point. BlackBerry's were a sign that one knew what one was up too. And Marc certainly knew what he was up too.

And so, it happened. Five bands from the compilation were asked to play. Billy Mahonie, Cove, Hirameka Hi Fi,

Reynolds, and Stanton.

The eleventh of December 2002, Chris from Reynolds' birthday. Tom from Hirameka put off travelling to Australia for four days to play it. He lost £400 in doing so. Flights were cheap to Australia back then.

We were to all get there for 4pm. Six hours before the show would start.

Chris Reynolds informed us that in the morning of the day we were currently having he had let a brown nerves packet plop into his undercrackers, and the undercrackers he was currently sporting were borrowed from Phil Reynolds. His neighbour's bin was the current home to his soiled set.

The toilets adjacent to Studio four were also receiving a sizeable dollop load from all.

We soundchecked. We went to the pub. We came back. We saw Paul Weller looking ridiculous and lost in the corridors. We were back in the studio for 9pm.

Peel strolled in at 9.10pm, bottle of wine and supermarket carrier bag full of records.

There was an audience. R1 had run a competition – "name another band from the comp other than the ones playing". The audience had responded and won the right to be there. The audience seemed to be made up of other bands from the compilation and Silver Rocket characters. There were beers and snacks.

Peel sat there, feet up on mixing desk, watching the five bands play, supping wine, tapping his toes. He gave a prize to the band who came closest to playing ten minutes, won by Reynolds. They went home with his trainers.

Due to the audience being there and us all being friends it

had felt like a gig.

To not put too fine a point on it, it was very excellent. And somehow, it'd worked out. And somehow, we'd survived. And somehow for one night only we felt like we were winning.

The following day I strolled into work, higher than a Creation Records band, to be brought back to earth by the fact that I worked in the part of the music industry that we were fighting against. No one had listened in. I checked to see if any online orders had come in from the previous night, they had. Piles of 'em. Vital had a franking machine. My boss Debbie was away. In no way did I abuse the work's franking machine.

And then on July 23, 2003, *it happened again.* Five bands from the second compilation had the same experience with Maida Vale and John Peel and wine in a carrier bag. Again, from *MORASRL:*

I recently emailed a man called Leon, who at the time lived in Tunbridge Wells: "Leon, you remember when Joeyfat and Bilge Pump and Charlottefield and I'm Being Good and Twinkie did the *10minutemen* session. Is it true that in TW there were 'radio parties'? outside? somewhere? or something….just doing this blog thing…trying to make it interesting…joe"

Leon replied:.

"Yes, we all ended up in a field in Chiddingstone in Kent with a few car radios blaring it out. I was there along with Lawrence and a few pals, we all ended up camping. I even drove a car for the first and last time, hand-brake turning into cow pats. When we woke up all the cows were in the field. It was a good evening!"

This Leon turns up later in the tale. Remember him.

So, we recorded our only Radio One session for Huw Stephens. We played a couple of songs from *II*: 'Take it' and 'Horsehead', the seven-inch song 'Ghost Ship', and a version of the Stereolab tune 'Noise of Carpet'. It was okay. It was broadcast on August the second, 2005. Phil from Victory Garden emailed and told me the seven-inch version was better and he was right.

We played around 20 more shows with Tim and Ian in the band before they left to go onto bigger and better things (i.e. not being in this band and not being in this band). These included our 50th show which was in Dalston at a short-lived venue called Bardens Boudoir which was underneath a Turkish restaurant. The venue was fifty metres by fifteen metres yet the stage was in the middle of the long side so thirty people could watch the band and 170 would be stuck out on the wings. Great venue, though. Saw US Maple in there. I'd dreamt of seeing that band. The band Blood Red Shoes played that night, they got big after this. Not on the back of this, but after this. A duo from Brighton, they accidentally signed to a major label. (ask them about this, it's not my place). Our claim to fame was that Jonson Family released their first seven-inch. In fact, we gave them their share of the seven-inch's at this show. It was a weird night, the night after 7/7*. The mood in London was a little downbeat but people showed up. We all wore white and had some projections going. We looked well East London, well arty.

We booked the venue. We made sure the bands got paid and we ended up having a decent time. Fifty was a milestone as it's a

---

* The 2005 co-ordinated suicide bomb attacks in London. Fifty-two UK residents of 18 different nationalities were killed, and more than 700 were injured.

plate spinning operation taking families and jobs and inclination into account. Any band who makes it to 50 shows deserves vast rewards. I probably mean the families deserve the rewards for putting up with it. Whatever, someone deserves rewards.

Tuesday May 31. Bardens, London, with Mae Shi, Rapider Than Horsepower, Bones Brigade, and Fading Fast.
Playing between two bands who like 'the mosh' meant we went down like a sack of shit. Watching the Bones Brigade singer try to kill the audience was funny. Mae Shi were arty, I quite liked them, RTH were a bit dull.

Ian:
DISEASE DISEASE SPREADING THE DISEASE, Bones Brigade started with Among the Living but stopped before the singing came in, disappointing. Bob did sound for everyone tonight except us, when no one did the sound. I gather we only sounded good from inside the toilets. Ah well. No James at this show and I feel he had the right idea. I liked Mae Shi, and Rapider. The one guitarist had a nice finger picking Magic Bandish style.

Tim:
This gig made me feel 100 years old. Like a Dad at the back of a concert hall waiting to pick up his kids. I think people were laughing at us. Didn't play too badly but still.

I have a feeling it was around this point that Tim decided that moving to Worthing would be a good idea and staying on in the band would be a bad idea. There's nothing like feeling ancient to bring you down. I bought a Bones Brigade record. It had a screen-printed sleeve and it totally rages but I like early Anthrax, so I would like it. They'd come over from the US to tour Europe. Somehow, American bands can come over to Europe and tour off the back of a DIY release, but the favour doesn't really get returned. This is for a couple of reasons: Their country is enormous so it's a bit off-putting for a band doing it off their own back, the cost of getting there is getting worse and worse, and, finally, the work visa issue is currently hurling a rammed bag of spanners into the works. The way round this is to go over with no instruments and do all you can to not look like a band, don't post any promotion on your websites, and maybe even travel separately. This avoids the visa issue, but not the flight cost and not the logistics of getting around a country that considers driving two hours for a loaf of bread absolutely reasonable.

It can take months for visas to get approved and it costs money to apply and you may not get the thing approved anyway, leaving any planned dates up the swanny and any money spent down the swanny. The damn swanny is now full of money and dates.

America doesn't want non-American underground bands. It has the Foo Fighters and The Killers already and that will do, thank you very much. Cheers America. We don't mind your bands coming over here. We quite like meeting people from other countries and expanding our minds with chats about the distance you drive to get bread and whatever else. You keep yourself to yourself, no worries. As I write this, the current keeper of the keys in that land is an orange cartoon character who got into power off the back of promising high walls and large racism. The chances of visas being waived for a band who have pressed 100 CDRs and can boast almost 500 Facebook likes is very slim. "You're stealing our DIY bands slots on a Tuesday night in Poughkeepsie, get out."

At the beginning of 2006, we did a six-date tour with Part Chimp, Todd, and Lords. We released a split ten-inch with all four bands on. We split it over the four labels who were dealing with the bands at the time – Rock Action, Southern, Gringo, and Jonson Family. A thousand copies were pressed, and it was a lot of fun. We played Glasgow, Leeds, Nottingham, Oxford, Brighton and London. The song we had on it was called 'On the Pleasure of Hating'. We played it correctly not one single time. Neither on the recording or live. It was way above our pay grade, littered with blast beats and slow bits and gruelling bits. You can tell the energy, though, and for that I give it three out of ten.

The last few shows with Tim on drums and Ian playing were decent.

Thursday June 2nd, 2006. 93 Feet East, London, with Oneida and Up C Down C
Tim:
Another opportunity to play with the masters Oneida. Frankly I think we'd travel anywhere in the UK to do it. We played a three-song (Take It, Europa, Noise Of Carpet) set that lasted 14 minutes. Would like to have played more. The second band were nice folks, two drummers, expensive guitars, sounded like Mogwai. Played for hours. The Oneida folks found the whole deal amusing. They rocked an *incredible* set. The drummer makes me want to sell my kit and become a potter or something.

Saturday June 11th, 2006. Ferryboat, Norwich, with Eaves and Bullet Union

I banged my head on the beams while we played, they were low. One chap yelled "shit" quite a lot while we were playing.

Tim:

Walked into pub to be greeted by some not very friendly looking skinheads (who would later all pile into pub's only cubicle to snaffle up some drugs). Pub did have nice cat though. Think its name was Black Witch or something. Met up with very friendly and super cool guys from Eaves. All the way from Aachen on the German, Belgium border. We really went down badly with some of the locals.

It is 8:01am. Leon Marks (guitar) is asleep in the living room. Rhys Llewellyn (drums) is asleep upstairs. I am in the kitchen with headphones on (Drab Majesty, in case you're interested). Paul Sykes (vocal) and Bob Davis (guitar) are asleep at Roo Farthings's (guitar) house twenty minutes away. We are in deep Somerset. It is Day Five in the studio and we are working on what will be our twelfth LP.

It's gone like this. For all you aspiring young bands out there wanting to get ahead in the music business, pay close attention. This is your Bible:

So far, we've had five sessions of just Roo and I in his loft coming up with loose ideas, recorded and sent round to the others. Totally loose, just a couple of ideas blu-tacked together, in need of a crack team to sort out and turn into actual songs. We've had four full band sessions at seven hours each. For these we've chosen a rehearsal room that is convenient for not one of us, in a place called Ashford (Middlesex) which is near Twickenham in extreme West London. It's pretty much the first clump of desolate housing you come across as you drive into London on the M3. Bleak expansive industrial roads, vast estates, no character. It always seems to be raining and there's virtually always a beautifully choreographed fight happening in and around the nearby Tesco. It's around two hours for us Somerset people and around an hour for the South East folk. The rehearsal room is nice. It's called Airplay and it's cheap as hell. About £40 for seven hours.

The first session Roo and I had was in September 2017. The first full band rehearsal was in October. Leon has recently rejoined after being away for five years, so we're bedding in a new guitarist. Doing it with new songs is the best way. Everyone's on the same page. We had two full band rehearsals then the first three days in the studio were booked for November 17th-19th. For this album we're recording in the city of Wells, in Somerset. This first session, unbeknown to us, was booked the same weekend as the Glastonbury and Wells carnivals.

If you're not from this area of Somerset you will have no idea about these. Carnival season is big round here; it travels around all the towns over the month of November. Groups of people spend the previous 12 months decorating the backs of flatbed lorries and trailers and floats with scenes (from nursery rhymes, or songs, or films, or real-life scenes – firemen, etc.) and then stand on the back of their flatbed lorry or whatever as it and hundreds of other flatbed lorries (or whatever) create a slow procession around the town. People set up stalls selling chips and bags of candy floss and other people bring flasks of tea and blankets and rain macs and stand around from around 6pm until 9pm watching all the flatbed lorries or whatever pass by. It's for charity. The lights are bright. The chip vans sell a lot of chips. We took Stan and Freddie to one of the first ones that happened when we moved down here. They ran around the petrol station by B&Q on the outskirts of Glastonbury for three hours, then we went home. It did, of course, rain. It always rains. But if they did it in the summer it wouldn't be dark, so the lights wouldn't look as good. In 2017 a flatbed lorry full of people in Bridgwater, standing still, creating their scene, had used the wrong light bulbs and all the people got burnt. They'd used tanning bulbs. It made the news. This is Somerset. You hit your thumb with a hammer and you're getting papped for a week.

Wells and Glastonbury were gridlocked for the weekend we recorded. We were all late and irritated. I had a wing mirror smashed off by a speeding delivery truck as everyone tore down tiny country lanes trying to find different routes. This area can't handle gridlock.

I want to call the album *Carnival*, I doubt anyone else does.

We recorded six songs over the first weekend. Roo and I had a couple more loft sessions and we had another two full band rehearsals – one in early December and one last weekend, the 21st January. And here we are, the 28th January 8.56am and I'm about to wake up Rhys and Leon and drive to Spacewolf Studios in Wells for day five. We have one song to record today and Paul will carry on working on the vocals. Yesterday we recorded four songs and bits of vocals.

When Metallica had a year, and then some, to record *St. Anger,* and could give the new bass player a million dollars for joining and could come up with almost entirely no music of worth in that year, it does make one scratch one's head. The Minutemen or Hüsker Dü recorded their greatest records over a couple of long weekends and were already playing the next album live when touring to promote them. It's a work ethic thing, a DIY culture thing, an art thing. In fact, if Metallica hadn't come out with *Some Kind of Monster,* one of the greatest music films of all time, then those 12 months would have been more than wasted. They would have been a crime against time. Someone in Mother Nature's Crime Investigation Unit would have knocked on Lars' door and said: 'Mate, those twelve months, you owe us, and you owe us *big*'.

Not that I'm comparing our skill level with that of Hüsker Dü or The Minutemen, but I'm not to Metallica either. So, you know.

Now it's 22.05pm, everyone's home. Probably in pieces. The day goes fast and slow and you achieve a lot but you're neither happy nor sad, you're just tired. Lord only knows. Maybe it'll all be on the cutting room floor by tomorrow.

Once *II* was out, and all the shows were done, Tim H and Ian left the band. Ian moved to Cambridge to save the world, or at least help with finding a cure for cancer. Tim moved to Worthing on the south coast and threatened to form a solo band called Poacher's Cap. We're still waiting for the results, you cannot rush it. To replace them we got three people in. Makes sense. Rhys Llewellyn joined on drums. He was part of the Shit and Shine drum team and was the only drummer in the Notorious Hi Fi Killers. Dave Briggs joined on guitar. He was from the band Cove. Dave was only in the band for eight shows. He turned up for five of them. The third new recruit was all round good guy and shuffling noise maker Duncan Brown, the Cosmic Leader. A bag of noise-making machines and a bottle of rum, that was our man Duncan.

The first thing we did with the new line up was record a single tune for a split twelve-inch with dot(.), a Japanese band of a extremely heavy nature. Our song was called 'Kittens'. We rehearsed and recorded at a studio called Dropout, in Camberwell down in South London, a hearty stroll from the Oval cricket ground and Camberwell High Street. In 2005 there were two kittens at Dropout, by 2006 there was one. Stuart survived, his mate didn't. We suspected he got plucked from the roof by a bird of prey, so we called the song 'Kittens', dedicated to the two of them. We didn't want the lost cat to be forgotten. Due to getting the taste for multi-label releases, three of them shared this release: Shifty in America, Blind Date out of Germany, and Jonson Family. This record even got re-pressed. Stunning. Ended up shifting around 1000 of these.

Dropout Studio was home for 10 or so years. We shared a rehearsal space and recorded everything from 2006 through to 2016 down there. Tim Cedar from Part Chimp and Jason Playford ran the place. As with all recording studios (that we use anyway), it's almost impossible to find. I've always assumed they don't want to advertise their whereabouts by doing anything as garish as having a sign, in case baddies break in and steal the kettle and mixing desk. Which of those two going missing would be felt more is hard to say. It was run in a haphazard fashion: a white board with scrawled bookings on; a phone that was never answered; texts that were rarely replied to. Always locked when we turned up, followed by a key hunt around South London. Every time we went in we seemed to catch the tail end of a 48-hour party. Grey-faced gurners spilling out blinking and crying into the sun as we strolled in to create our hellish din. It's amazing Stuart the cat survived it all; he was an enthusiast. We loved it. It was good for us and the atmosphere was perfect for what we were doing. It may not have been perfect for a traditional covers band, but for what we were up to it captured it perfectly. Jason and Tim were (are) splendid souls and the sound we got, and most other bands got down there, was very correct. Somewhere online you can watch Bardo Pond playing live in the basement. Earth did some work in there. Evan Dando, a whole host of characters. I think even Florence and the Machine started off there.

The song 'I am the Chiswick Strangler' was part of a pile of songs we recorded down Dropout for our third album. Tim Cedar recorded it. We called the album Project:Death, this title stuck because Rhys scrawled it onto rough mix CDRs he'd handed round to us all to check out at home. The joke stuck. Chris Summerlin came up with the sleeve, him from Lords, him from Reynolds, etc, etc. It was a meat cleaver with blood dripping off. The whole thing was funny to us. We were being lumped in with doom bands and metal bands and all the shows we played outside of London were with doom and metal bands. I love doom and metal as much as the next man, assuming the next man quite likes doom and metal. But, god damn, we played with them all. Some of them ruled hard. There was a band from Glasgow called Snowblood, for instance, who would crush us every time we played with them. Precision and passion, they were total monsters. Black Sun, also from Scotland were excellent. But often the bands we played with were image over content and in the end it drove us crazy.

As proof of my love of the heft I was asked to write words for the Louder Sound website, 10 records that influenced. Classic list stuff. A couple I included:

Godflesh - Pure
This came out the day before my eighteenth birthday, and I bought it because I'd seen Mike Patton wearing the *Streetcleaner* T-Shirt. There you go – owning up. It took a big MTV star to make me discover a band from 100 miles up the road. I was doing work experience in central London, so had to catch a train into town, with my cassette Walkman as protection. Something my dad used to say: "Tape your records, then play the tape rather than wear the record out!" So, I immediately taped *Pure*, and it was the only

tape I listened to for two weeks, going into Soho, and home again. The sound and visuals are etched in my brain. Such a monster of a record, each time I listen to it (as I am right now, on vinyl – the cassette is long gone) I FEEL the train chuntering into Euston, through north London. This and *Streetcleaner* are untouchable. Mike Patton taught me to stop listening to what the mainstream was telling me to listen to – so I stopped listening to his band. We played with JK Flesh at Supersonic Festival in 2012. I told no one, but it felt like a full circle moment.

Anthrax - Among The Living
My favourite record by the big four. It has zest and is positive, lyrically and in spirit, and mixes it up like a NYHC record. Scott Ian's rhythm guitar is absolutely and utterly terrifyingly on point, and the bass at the beginning of Caught In A Mosh, YESSSSS! In fact, Frank Bello's bass all the way through is so prominent it runs the show. I initially bought it on cassette in Our Price, Hemel Hempstead, but soon swapped it for the vinyl version, and have owned it now for almost thirty years and it still tears it up. We all went to see them on the *State Of Euphoria* tour at Hammersmith Odeon, by this time they were wearing Bermuda shorts and looked like the Red Hot Chili Peppers, but we kind of forgave them. I drifted away from them, but always knew I loved this record and would occasionally dig it out on drunken nights. Then, a couple of years ago my son, aged sixteen, said to me: "I like Slayer and Anthrax." Seconds later we had tickets to see both bands in Birmingham (I paid a few pounds more to get a physical ticket, you gotta have gig tickets to look back on. What are people gonna look at in years to come? Emails? Good grief) and watching both bands with him almost made me cry. Time

had passed, he was my age when I discovered them, I'd had and lost jobs, bought a house, got married, and there we were sitting at the back of the venue, staring down at the mosh pit going crazy, and he had a look in his eyes that said 'I WILL NEVER FORGET THIS', and I had a look in my eyes that said 'I WILL NEVER FORGET THIS'. Then we got a £40 parking ticket and drove home.

I have a metal background, a metal youth. I like it. I think we all just wished the bills were more mixed up. Anyhow.

One of the weekends we recorded *P:D* (it was recorded over a couple of weekends in December 2006) we played two shows. I cannot fathom why we thought this was a good idea. If you're in a band then do not do this and if you have done this, my money is you regretted it.

Saturday December 2nd, 2006. Oval, Dropout, with Kling Klang
We recorded on the Friday night and through Saturday then played in the studio in the evening. We were a bit shit. But it was fun. Amp probs, tiredness, and more tiredness. KK rocked it up with keyboards galore.

Sunday December 3rd, 2006. Stockwell, London, The Grosvenor with Monno and Todd
Question: is Todd's album one of the best from 2006? Answer: YES. Simple innit. Go see them if you get the chance as they give a night to remember. Monno were inspirational as well, rhythm v sax v big sound + laptops = new meaning to heavy. A very enjoyable Sunday night. Which surprised me as I was half blind due to smashing my glasses up at the previous night's gig, so I

couldn't actually see anything.

This weekend was not helped by the glasses issue. The first night we played in the studio, it was recorded and supposed to end up as a live record. It was so bad it got scrapped. On the tube home that evening, I thought I was having a stroke or my brain was falling apart in some other manner as my left eye had all but gone blind. Poking myself in the eye to see what was going on I discovered that the glass had fallen out of the frame and instead of my finger stopping at the glass it went straight through to my open eye. I hope I'm not the only person to ever do this. My fellow passengers heading northbound on the Victoria Line managed to keep that London cool in place and utterly ignore my situation. I don't know if London has changed recently but the London of mid-noughties was a cold, hard place.

'I am the Chiswick Strangler' is arguably the banger from the album. It races through like The Damned or maybe even the band Leatherface. It's a song Bob brought the parts for. Bob's strength is the banger. His songs are very route one, and all bands need some route one action in their set. A tune that bypasses the midfield. Get it up there, let the big forward hoof it home. Consequently, of course, it was fun to play live. If your set is full of 10-minute slabs of downtuned sounds set to crush, you need to mix it up with some ragers.

(If you're unaware of the art of the downtuned guitar then it goes along these lines – the standard western tuning for a six-string guitar is EADGBE, Eat Apples Daily Grow Big Ears. If you're a mean metal band (Slayer) or a noise rock band (Unsane) or a chin stroking art rock band (Sonic Youth) then you must tune your guitar differently as you wouldn't want to be the same as the Edge (U2) or him from Coldplay (Coldplay). The theory is it opens the guitar to 'new opportunities, maaaaaaaan' so you can play lower, therefore heavier, or more discordant and 'original'. Of course, only one per cent of the audience care about this but you go through the motion purely in the hope that that one per cent comes up to you after the show and asks you about it.)

Playing 'Chiswick' (as it was written on all the set lists) was fun. There's footage on YouTube of us doing it at the Gringo Records 10th birthday up in Nottingham and someone very audibly shouts: 'BUY A TUNER'. In fact, after this show Rhys and Jon Hamilton from Part Chimp, who also played, got straight into Rhys' car and drove to Paris to play with Shit and Shine the next night. I believe they made it with seconds to spare. This is exactly the sort of behaviour I encourage. You got some seconds to spare then drive to Paris and play with Shit and Shine. No excuses. Also, after the Gringo 10th Birthday, we went out and bought tuners. I also encourage this. I think if we had owned tuners from the beginning, say from 1986, we would have saved ourselves a total of two years in wasted time.

Project:Death was released on vinyl by Wakusei. They pressed 300 copies. Simon Rowson and Heather Weil, who ran the label, are both lovely people. They also put shows on in and around North London at the time, mainly using The Swan in Tottenham. A lot of incredible underground punk shows happened here. It's around five miles north of central London. People travelled to this venue, it built a reputation. Curried goat always bubbling away. Kids running around. Soundsystem in the front bar. The sound was great when fifty people were in there and when it was packed, it was electric. Our tenth ever show was at the Swan:

Monday January 19th 2004 . The Swan, Tottenham, with Wolves and Transistor Transistor.

Due to the ex-Orchid nature of Wolves this was a very busy night at The Swan. I thoroughly enjoyed both other bands but for the life of me I had no idea which was which. They both sounded identical to my ears. I ended up getting their split twelve-inch on Level Plane and it's turned out to be one of my most played records. It's good going out music.

Ian:

The other two bands were almost indistinguishable from one another in their screamy hardcoreness. TOP rating on the curry goat smell for this show though. NICE.

James:

Liked Wolves, or was it Transistor Transistor?? Liked the reggae in the bar more, mind you.

And being a DIY show in a venue that was free to hire and put on by people who weren't interested in making money, it still stands in our top five shows in regards getting paid. We were almost embarrassed. The combination of selling our just-released record (*Hates You*) and the generous pay pretty much financed the recording of our next album.

Here's Simon Rowson, from Wakusei Records, talking about booking The Swan, and sorting shows in North London:

"I never understood why the Swan put up with us. I think it had a lot to do with Chris Thackaberry (a London promoter from the 1990s and into the 2000s) who built up the relationship there before I got involved with booking bands. It was always slightly ramshackle and disorganised (maybe I'm just ramshackle and disorganised). I'm sure those kind of shows still are to some degree. People were slightly freaked out about travelling to Tottenham then - it wasn't in Zone One or Two and there was nothing much else around there. Venues were sparse. Well, venues willing to put on the kind of bands we were booking anyway. If the band was good or well known people would travel, as I discovered to varying degrees of success. Outside of the Swan we were stuck with places like the Verge, upstairs at the Garage or the odd pub who would agree to putting on a show then get pissed off and not let us book there again. The only other reliable venues I can remember at that time was the Grosvenor, Bardens Boudoir and an Aussie pub in Kings Cross. For whatever reason the Swan didn't mind, they didn't give a shit what the music was like as long as people were buying drinks from the bar.

My memory is dreadful but I can still recall the regulars playing their twerking videos on a projector in the back room and the animated domino matches out the front while we were trying to set up shows somewhere in-between the two. The high points for me were the shows that were so rammed the walls were dripping with sweat and the place was buzzing. It proved things can happen and happen successfully outside zones 1 and 2. Whenever I booked DS-13 it would be like that, the same for any of those Deranged Records bands. Brutal Knights, The Oath, Tear It Up, etc. More than these though I loved the UK bands I put on as there was more of a connection. You could see them grow, knew them better, saw them more often. I still play that The! Lights! Alive! demo from time to time".

The!Lights!Alive! were a very young band from Highams Park, just outside Walthamstow. The only song they released was on the

TwoMinutemen compilation Jonson Family put out. Their demo did the rounds though. They were excellent live. Not sure why they didn't go on to release an album. All the members went on to great and good things. Simon goes on:

> "The flip side were the ones that almost went completely wrong, I think it was Kaospilot from Norway where we turned up to get everything ready and the place had been double booked. After some wrangling we managed to get them to agree to us setting it all up in the corner of the pub instead. I remember the locals playing the fruit machine next to the stage while a Norwegian screamo band were going wild next to them. It was completely surreal. There were a couple of complete disasters; I think one may have even involved Hey Colossus. Again, the venue had been double booked (towards the end so many people were trying to book shows there it must have been a nightmare for them to keep on top of it all). I turned up and had to find another venue at the last minute, no playing in the corner of the pub this time. I can't remember how we found it but there was a pub in Dalston with a stage in the corner willing to let us use it. We put it out on social media the venue had changed about an hour before the show, left someone at The Swan to redirect people and raced to the new venue to get set up. Inevitably the show was sparsely attended and I'm sure I lost money on it but at least we sorted something out for the band.*
>
> Most of the other nightmares would have been along similar lines. PAs not turning up or bands getting lost so shows

---

* This was a show with Snowblood from Scotland. We have no memory of it being a disaster. It happened. That is always the main thing.

not starting til 10 or 11 at night and dealing with irate people who had travelled for the show and had to miss the band. The bands getting lost was a recurring theme, especially for touring bands outside of the UK. They would assume, as the show was in London, it would be central, so drive to somewhere like Oxford Street and be like 'hey where's the venue?'. I'd then have to explain how to get to Tottenham from central London while pulling my hair out about nothing being ready yet".

Why did you do Wakusei, when were you active, why did you stop?
"Wakusei started around 2000, I'd finished university, moved back to London and started working a crappy data job but it did mean I had some disposable income at last. Releasing records seemed like a natural progression to me from the love of buying vinyl (mainly thanks to places like Hot Rocks in Sutton and Shake Some Action/Beanos in Croydon when I was at school) to then playing in and booking bands. I'm sure it's the same for most labels. You see a band and something about them grabs you and you want to be associated with them in some way, there's a certain joy in hearing a great record and thinking "I released that".

The label was never a business; I didn't make any money on anything I released. If I was lucky they would make costs back so I could release something new. I always had a day job and the label always took second place to that. I guess personal commitments became more important than injecting my own money into keeping the label going, perhaps some of the fun had gone. This would have been around 2009".

Who or what were your influences for running the label and putting shows on?

"Sean Forbes was a huge influence, I can remember having ordered records from his label and distro for a couple of years then being 19 with a dreadful demo tape for my own band naively approaching him to see if he was interested in releasing it.* He said in the nicest possible way do it yourself, here is a list of places to press records, places to master it etc. The knowledge that it was that easy and people were so open to help was incredible.

The same with putting on shows, places like the Tap and Casbah in Edinburgh in the late 1990s. Going there, meeting people, helping out, then putting shows on yourself. Just the punk / diy community and network was inspiring. It's not without its problems but the good parts are great and the realisation you can play/write/record/promote/tour on your own and there's a network of people to help you do that is just incredible".

Three records you'd save from a fire Simon?

"Oh wow, this probably changes on a daily basis depending on my mood. Right now it would be New Order - *Power, Corruption and Lies*; Manuel Gotsching - *E2-E4;* and Spacemen 3 - *Recurring* (who doesn't love a 10-minute pop song?)"

* Sean Forbes is a larger than life chap, Rough Trade Records basement dweller, ran the label Rugger Bugger, played in Wat Tyler, plays in Hard Skin

The CD version of *Project:Death* was released by Shifty Records in America, Underhill in Spain, Jonson Family in the UK and Rimbaud in Ireland. All the label logos on the back of the sleeve, it looked beautiful (we thought). Due to the number of labels involved and them all wanting a reasonable amount, the scale of economy of making CDs ensured that we could make a lot of them and the cost barely budged. To this day, this CD still ticks over at shows. It's down to a fiver now but we pressed so many that we'll probably never run out.

The art for the vinyl versions of *II* and *Project:Death* were both different to their CD compatriots. This is abnormal behaviour. A multinational corporation would advise against this. The marketing would be about one image. All formats would need to have that image. Sell the image, god damn it. Heather Weil created new art for both, wildly different imagery, so I asked her about that.

"We always tried to make packaging interesting for our releases at Wakusei but on a shoestring budget. With *Project:Death,* I had wanted to make letterpress covers, but ended up using stamps and embossing powder and spent a couple of summer days sitting in the garden with a glue stamp pad, the embossing powder and a hairdryer. There were a handful of limited versions where Simon hand drew some of his goofy illustrations on manila office envelopes. Wakusei releases were always fun to make. With *II* I had a little more freedom to make a cover. In listening to *II* there's a maelstrom of angular stoner sludge with swirly yet crushing psychedelia. I wanted the design to balance with the music. At the time that we released *Project:Death* and *II*, I was listening to a lot of the Vertigo Records catalogue, German Oak, Flower Travellin Band, Killed by Death punk classics and a solid staple of many years prior and since, the Party of Helicopters *Please Believe It* record'.

I was interested in what was going on for Heather now:
"Soon after Wakusei ended I hooked up musically with Kevin Morpurgo and at that time Matt Ridout,* and the three of us started Black Impulse which at the time was show booking, mixes and hanging out and being idiots. Somehow, we ended up with a show on NTS (nts.live). Apparently, people listen to it, which is always shocking to me. Almost seven years later, Kev and I are still in the studio every other week, playing new heaviness and old classics. Kev is putting on shows in Margate and London now as Connect Nothing with Nothing."

And because I know you're interested, because I know I am, here's three records Heather would save:
"Yasuaki Shimizu – *Kakashi.* I was very lucky and copped an original some time ago with obi strip. It's a perfect record and I am glad it finally got the recognition it deserves. I always play 'Yume Dewa' out, and whenever I do have people asking what it is I point them in the direction of the Palto Flats *WRWTFWW* repress. *Total Issue* [self-titled]. Dreamy French prog which took almost a year to arrive from the seller, but 'La Porte Ouverte' has become a Black Impulse classic.

* Both Kevin and Matt were in Dethscalator, who HC released a split twelve-inch with. Both are still doing music, Casual Sect and Casual Nun respectively. Two Casual bands, Coincidence I assume.

William Sheller, *Lux Aeterna*, A masterpiece from start to finish; psychedelic classical with full choir, shredding guitars, the sparse vocal pieces are very similar to some elements of Aphrodite's Child 666 or Magma, but set against a full orchestra. Truly stunning. Like *Total Issue*, a record I rarely leave home without when I'm playing out or doing Black Impulse"

The slightly disappointing part about *Project:Death* is that it doesn't quite sound like we wanted it too. The recording was great, but I think as a band we'd all agree that the mix and mastering wasn't quite up to scratch and for that we take full responsibility. We did it ourselves and we shouldn't have. The songs are decent enough and for a fiver you shouldn't complain. No refunds. It was a lesson learned.

Mastering is a mysterious art, it happens after the recording has been mixed. It's done to ensure all the sounds cut through and all the song volumes are similar. It can bring out tones yet unheard. It can bring to life a record, it can make it louder. For instance, when you hear an Oasis song on the radio and it's one of their all guns blazing tunes, it's weirdly hard to hear it. The song has been mastered so loud that it's created a wall of noise. If it wasn't for Liam's voice over the top you'd think it was a team of cement mixers churning away. All the subtlety has been sucked out purely to make it sound louder than all other music and more anthemic than all other music. It seems like it was purely done to destroy every other tune on the radio. Mastering can cost thousands of pounds if you're Oasis in the 1990s or it can be way more reasonable if you hunt around. We were guilty on *P:D* of cutting costs and doing it ourselves and we got a little stung. We've since done some hunting. We now use Part Chimp Jon. He is excellent.

We pay him in a currency that I'm not allowed to write about.

For this record we toured Spain. We toured Spain because Underhill Records released the album in that country and they sorted the shows for us. We toured Spain because we really wanted to play outside of the UK and the idea of going to a hot country appealed. We didn't realise how far Spain is away from the UK, and how big Spain is, and how much driving you need to do to get all the way through France.

16th October

We wake in Rhys's South London flat, 4am. We have someone driving us. His name is Jon Wood, he's now a very successful businessman running his own very successful business called Ooosh! Tours. His business is vans for bands and vans are big business in the band world. We drive to Dover to catch the 9am ferry. We drive to Poitiers, a town halfway down France. Terrible traffic, 90 minutes of being totally still just south of Paris. We get there at 9.15pm and load into the venue, an Irish Bar called Buck Mulligans. We're opening for Mothertrucker, a band from the Midlands. A band with some lovely folk in who to this day we still bump into every now and then. One shared microphone for Bob and Paul, they look like a 1980s hair metal band, singing into each other's eyes. The crowd, already drunk, are stunned. We get paid 70 euros and 10 UK pounds.

17th October

Poitiers to Valencia is just over 1000km. We're up at 4am for the second day and drive and drive and drive, getting to the venue at 9pm. 16 people pay to get in. The police stop the show halfway through as the venue isn't 100 per cent legal and the noise is proving too horrific for the locals. An excellent day.

18th October

Jon the driver leaves the flat to go and get the van which was parked around a few corners. The night before, parking wasn't fun. We had to circle the promoters flat a few times to get a spot. There's no Hollywood parking in Valencia, the way a space is always available for the protagonist. Race around the city, scream into a spot right outside whatever place it is, no worries. Parking is easy in Hollywood films. Hollywood films would be twice as long if Statham or Gibson had to find a spot to park before performing their punching and running and sexing. Old European cities are traditionally a total nightmare to park in. In a Mercedes Sprinter the nightmare is doubled and becomes a living hellish reality. I have a friend from Turin. He told me the city of Turin has so many cars that it would be impossible for them all to find a parking space if, indeed, they all wanted to park at the same time. The city relies on a decent percentage of its drivers to be on the road at all times. Valencia surely has a similar system in place. Jon the driver was taking too long, he wasn't back in ten minutes or twenty or thirty minutes. Our host, the promoter from the previous night's show, had to go to work so we had to get out of the house. We were now standing on the pavement. The weather being decent was a blessing. After around an hour we got a message from Jon, he had lost the van and had left the Sat Nav in the flat. Luckily we had his bag so consequently had his Sat Nav. An hour later he phoned. He'd found the van and instead of trying to find the flat had driven to a landmark and we should all walk to him. The walking began. We typed in his location, a museum, and began the trek. Being new to both satellite navigation and Valencia we didn't realise we were walking the route the way a vehicle would have to take. We were looping around blocks in the way a car would when obeying the one-way systems. Twenty minutes would pass, and we'd be back at the same spot to then head off up a different road. From Jon leaving us to us getting to the van took five hours. We fought, split up, shouted, abused each other and everyone nearby. Tensions were off the hook.

Around this time, back home, Elisa and my two very young boys (Stan, seven, and Freddie, four) were moving to our new house. From London to Somerset. I should have been there. I'd driven all our stuff down in a seven-and-a-half-tonne lorry before heading to Spain. It turns out that if you passed your driving test in 1991 you could drive these massive beasts, so we moved ourselves. Elisa rang to say someone had just smashed one of our front windows, a local sending a message. At this point, with Bob and James and Rhys shouting at everything that moved or shouting at things until they moved – lamp posts, fire hydrants, shops – I was on the verge of getting a cab home.

We found the van, got a pile of cans, and sat in silence. It only took a beer and a smoke and some gentle ribbing of Jon to ease the agony. We drove to Madrid and played an average show with Moho and Adrift. Adrift, also with Underhill Records in Spain, were to be our tour buddies for the rest of the tour.

It turned out the smashed window at home was a window slamming in the wind. At the time, coupled with the stress of moving, it was almost enough to send things spiralling. Elisa is, luckily for me, a very accepting person. I proposed to her while cooking some Cauldron Veggie sausages (I heartily recommend these with beans and mash. A meal from your childhood. Only now with no pig toe nails, horse fingers or cow anus included) in our flat in Wood Green in 2000. This was considered OK. We got married eight weeks later in a registry office in Enfield. Around thirty friends came and we all went to get pizza in Palmers Green, at a restaurant called Rimini. They made us a cake, it said: "Happy Wedding" in icing on the top. We're yet to have a honeymoon. She has to listen to my hare-brained ideas day after day, around one in a hundred are plausible. Starting this band was one of the implausible ones.

19th October

Bilbao with Adrift. I bought the *Very Hungry Caterpillar* book in Basque and pointlessly gave it to Freddie when I got home. It must be in the house somewhere. What a great city Bilbao is. Escalators take people up steep hills. These are needed because of Kalimoxto, a mixture of red wine and cola. Kalimoxto is not a hill climber's friend yet is very popular in the very hilly city of Bilbao. The venue was built into the hill, we loaded in on the bottom floor and took the lift up six flights to get to the ground floor. This was easily the best show of the tour. Enough people came to make it worthwhile and because of the way a lot of venues are funded in Europe we got paid enough to go a long way to covering the costs of the tour. We still lost money, don't get me wrong. If your first tour of Europe makes you money you're doing it all wrong. The key is to keep going back, eventually you win people over. Or not. Either way it's an adventure.

20th October

We liked Bilbao so much we pulled out of the show booked for this night just to stay near the city. It was Adrift's idea to pull out of it. They said it was too far and would be a wash out. It didn't take much to convince us. We were staying in a log cabin in the woods above the city with a bubbling fire and both bands hanging out. It was like being in the 1937 version of Heidi but instead of Heidi and her grandad in Switzerland it was ten grotty men up in the hills. The sun peeking through the trees, coffee pot on the boil, in beautiful Spain. It didn't matter that not many people were coming to the shows, it was idyllic and to this day I genuinely think these moments are worth the fight. The music is important, the people you're with are important, the way you get through things is vital, the fact you've succeeded or failed from your own actions is poetic. I bore people with this. I bore myself with this. If you build something yourself and it hits one person in a positive manner, it's about the most you can get out of life. Not much else matches it. I get that selling ten million records must be incredible or headlining the main stage at Reading Festival is something that you'd cling onto forever, but it's the little things. The seeds you plant.

21st October
Gijon on a Sunday night, like many places on a Sunday night, is not very good for gigs.

22nd October
The start of the massive drive home with a sleep stop in Bordeaux as our friends from Leeds, the splendid Bilge Pump, were playing. We got pulled over as we went across the border. The French police let a dog go through the van. I'm pretty sure I saw it being sick as we drove away from it. The poor mutt wouldn't have lasted a second longer sniffing through our debris; a week of dirty pants, beer bottles and other bottles with suspicious undrinkable liquid. Us five showing up at the Bilge Pump show more than doubled the attendance. Turns out that Bordeaux on a Monday

night, like many places on a Monday night and like Gijon on a Sunday night, is not very good for gigs. It was good to see some fellow road warriors though. We stayed over and then on the 23rd we drove the one-hundred-million miles back to the UK.

Did we in any way succeed in promoting the band during this tour? Did we in any way help shift some units on this tour? Did we in any way make money on this tour? No. No. And, of course, no. Can I explain the attraction of such a week to people who don't do this sort of thing? Nope. I could try but I wouldn't be able to make the idea stick. It is what it is. If it doesn't in any way sound attractive to you, meeting new people, seeing new things, learning about playing to people in faraway places, getting around the problems, getting lost then getting found, then it's not going to be for you.

Five years after the beginning of this band. Twenty-two years after beginning playing music in groups. Thirty-four years after being born. For the first time, a label not run by us releases an album we're doing. CD only for now, you have a nine-year wait for the vinyl version. Riot Season is based in the town of Willenhall in the middle of England. It's one man, his name is Andy Smith and some people think he doesn't exist. We know bands who have released records on Riot Season who have never met Andy. He released two albums by the (very) rock group Bad Guys and they never once set eyes on him. Then they split up so will almost certainly never meet him. I knew he existed.

For around eight years I worked in the 'music business'. For three months I worked for free at Southern, a record distributor for a lot of the alt.rock record labels out of America - Dischord, Touch and Go, Skin Graft - and a few decent UK labels like Crass Records and Wiiija. Southern was also a record label and had a recording studio in Wood Green. As a company it had helped bands like Rudimentary Peni get their records into shops and was a big part of the UK underground through the eighties and into the nineties. I was on the dole so working for free made sense, I thought. I wanted to get into working in the world I enjoyed the most. The three months I worked in their Haringey warehouse on an industrial estate in between Crouch End and Turnpike Lane was, as I look back now, very enjoyable. I can still smell the rotten fruit and veg in the fridge, I can still smell the shrink-wrapping machine, I can still not feel my fingers as the vast doors were always open for vans to drop off and pick up. There were six other people working in the label's warehouse, our job was to ship records to distributors around Europe and provide restocks to bands who were on tour.

The other characters working there were all in bands. All three of the punk band Broccoli worked for Southern in one form or another. A couple of the people from the experimental indie krautrocky band Quickspace worked there (my stag do involved myself, Simon and Bob going to see them on Tottenham Court Road and then going home to bed early). Ben from Thatcher On Acid (Somerset based anarcho band from the 1980s) and Hard Skin (an Oi band, sort of. Not a joke, but sort of a joke. I have no idea. They sing about darts and cars and Millwall even though none of them support Millwall. They're funny to people not into Oi and the people into Oi seem fifty per cent furious at them for once having long hair, and fifty per cent into them for being excellent) also worked there.

I spent two whole weeks jamming Shellac's second record, *Terraform*, into its sleeve. We then waited forty-eight hours for Steve Albini, the band's furiously right-on but very entertaining frontman, to decide which way round he wanted the outer sleeve inserted into the PVC protector. Our job was inner sleeve into outer sleeve, then outer sleeve into PVC protector. Half of the records in circulation have my blood on. Have a look in your copy, grab my DNA. If you're reading this in 2327 then re-create me.

I'm decent at cooking and I brush my teeth twice daily, I'm quite a catch. The sleeves to *Terraform* were brutally unforgiving. They were tough. I performed this task with a black-metal goth whose name has long escaped me, he was from Florida and wore black, black and more black. Must have had a whale of a time in the Florida sun.

The other very memorable mission was the mass destruction, for tax purposes I assumed at the time, of thousands of CDs and records and tapes. Which, now as we head well into the 21st century, I see being reissued by all sorts of labels. We could make off with what we wanted. I, and everyone who I thought would be interested, ended up with all The Didgits, Laughing Hyenas and Pegboy records. It hurt, doing this task, and baffled. Records don't need to eat, storing them is easy, tuck them away for a rainy day. That's my tip for you thinking of selling off your C-list grunge records, your eighties hair metal, your early 2000s post-hardcore records. Keep them. Put them in a box. One day you'll be grateful.

A couple of miles away in Tottenham was where the main distribution was based. It was called SRD (Southern Record Distribution). It shipped records to shops in the UK and to other record distributors around Europe for them to ship to the shops in their countries. After three months at Southern I got an actual paying job here. It was almost £10,000 a year. Really excellent for London, assuming the year was 1889. SRD distributed a wide variety of music, not just Southern Records material. It covered decent reggae on Greensleeves Records, Drum and bass from labels like Full Cycle, and big house/dance releases on Global Underground. Back in the days of CDs selling by the bucketload shops like HMV took roughly millions of the Global Underground albums. They were all mix CDs by heavy-hitting DJs and we found them hilarious. Huge pallets would turn up of these things, we'd ship them to HMV who would then smash half of them and return them on another huge pallet. Money must have been changing hands, but I have no idea who was doing well, it was a revolving door of CDs with DJs faces on. Half the people working in SRD were taking ecstasy and skipping around the aisles. 45% of the people working there were moody spliff toking BMW three Series driving drum and bass bad boys from Tottenham. The last 5% were people like me, essentially boring and trying to not make mistakes while being hungover. The hours of eleven to seven suited.

The warehouse was run by a man called Penguin, he wore white trousers and had metal plates in his head. He'd taken a beating somewhere or other, he was a nice man. I have no idea why he got the beating. I guess not everyone likes white trousers. His car had the number plate SRD N17, the job and the postcode were important to him. He gave me the job and I will never hear a bad word said about him. I also don't know why he was called Penguin, unless, as with the beating, the white trousers were to blame.

After a year here I moved to Vital, a different distribution company. This one was based in Ladbroke Grove, entirely the other side of the city. The two grand pay rise was eaten up, and then some, by the leap in travel costs. It was here I first started talking to Andy Smith of Riot Season, although at the time Riot Season didn't exist. He ran a record shop, an online shop, called Chunky. He doesn't know I first started talking to him back then. I was on telesales, phoning shops up and trying to get them to take a zillion copies of the Baha Men's 'Who let the Dogs out' CD single. From Shellac to the Baha Men in a year. My head was in my hands.

It was at Vital where I met Tim, HC's first drummer, also Duncan who joined at the tail end of Tim's time and first put his sounds on the *Project:Death* album. I put a lot of stock in being in bands with friends. You can tell a lot by someone when watching them make a cup of tea. There are rules. Over a year or two of monitoring this you get the vibe of a person.

Through working first at SRD then at Vital I met a lot of good people, many people I'm still in touch with. Some I've been best man for. Some I've waited in a pub for five hours for, on Christmas day, while their housemates attempt to climb out of Ketamine-related slumps. Elisa was working that day. She's a midwife. I was seeing family people over the next few days. I wasn't being a bad son or boyfriend. I was brought up a catholic, the guilt would have killed me. It seemed like an excellent idea to spend the day in a Wetherspoons in Manor House once the opportunity presented itself. A break from the norm, something for a future book.

It was through meeting Marc at SRD, as mentioned in the John Peel story earlier, that we got that break. It was while working for free at Southern and meeting all the people there and seeing them going off on tour that it occurred that it was all do-able, you didn't need to be signed to Geffen.

When I first spoke to Andy Smith he had a record label called Resonant. They were releasing records by post-rock bands like Do Make Say Think and Kepler. The label was run by himself and another Andy, Andy Slocombe.

I knew Andy Smith was a decent person with incredibly dry Black Country humour. When his new label started, Riot Season, he was soon releasing records by Acid Mothers Temple and Circle. These bands were big deals in the world of freewheeling guitar abusers. Both are still thundering along now, doing better than ever before. In fact, in 2017 Circle released their biggest record yet, on Southern Lord, the label ran by Stephen O Malley, the big amp owner from the doomy drone band Sunn0))). It seems all the bands in this world, Circle, Acid Mothers, even us, don't really have a plan. There's no well thought-out spreadsheet with the next three years planned out. I used to think we were playing the long game, one day people will come around to us. But now I don't think we're playing a game at all. We're writing music and recording music and releasing music and playing live and it's just what it is. That's it. My guess is if I took a straw poll amongst everyone we know, all who we meet when going about our business, they would all say the same. We're in a different beautiful world, away from those that are aiming for the headline slot at Bestival or T in the Park. If you're my mum and you've read this far, this is the one thing to take away from all these words. We're in a parallel world, the upside down.

Seeing as Andy was kind enough to release our music, I thought perhaps it'd be fair to let him explain himself. Especially as some people think he doesn't exist.

When and why did Resonant start?
"We started Resonant in 1998. At that time, and for the year before I'd started selling records via mail order for a living under the banner of Chunky Records. I'd had a bout of illness which laid me off my day job for three months or so. During that time off the company changed hands and I was made redundant and for no apparent reason I thought 'I'll start selling records to get by.

I can't remember any logical reason for deciding that, other than being an avid record buyer and music lover from the age of eight when I first discovered rock music.

I'd got zero experience in any form of buying or selling records and it was a total step in the dark. I was thinking 'If I buy five copies of this LP or CD and sell four, I'll get my own copy for free', and so Chunky Records was born. One of the distributors/suppliers I dealt with for stock were SRD in London. I got to know the folks there and friendships formed, and this eventually led to the idea of doing a label together with one of them. We liked a lot of the same current music I was selling (and he was distributing) and hated a lot of each other's favourites as well. We settled on a middle ground which was loosely post-rock and a bit of electronica.

I'd never even thought about running a record label up to that point in my life. I barely even knew what it even entailed. But from selling other labels stuff and working with distributors it didn't look that difficult. One of the biggest selling labels for my mail order were Constellation Records from Canada. I got their stuff via SRD and struck up a dialogue with the label owners and used to get heads up on new stuff. I think I was one of the first UK based outlets to sell Godspeed You Black Emperor's first album, I sold tons of that, and then another Constellation band called Do Make Say Think came up on our radar. I can't recall the exact details of how we came to do the debut Resonant release with them. I think we asked them cheekily when we heard they were coming over to the UK. It made sense for them to have something else out there to promote/sell, so we ended up doing a twelve-inch EP of four-track recordings called *Besides*. I think we pressed 1000 copies and sold them all pretty quickly. That was the start of Resonant as a label. My biggest regret about the whole Resonant period was not being able to convince Do Make Say Think to let us reissue the twelve-inch with a better sleeve or bonus tracks. We did have the extra tracks but we'd used just four to make it a twelve-inch single. It was too soon after their debut album to release another full length record".

Why switch to doing Riot Season?

"As time rolled on with Resonant, the chance came up to do a record with Japanese band Acid Mothers Temple. Another UK distributor called Harmonia Mundi used to sell me their P.S.F. label releases and I was intrigued by the weird looking people on the covers not just the music. One conversation led to another and before long, and without any experience, I was booking a full UK/Irish tour for AMT [May 2001). We were also putting out a double album called *Absolutely Freak Out (Zap Your Mind)* as a co-release with another Midlands based label called Static Caravan, who I knew via promoting Birmingham shows with its owner Geoff. We released this under the banner 'Staticresonance' and followed it up with other releases from the likes of Circle, Nishinihon and Brain Donor (Julian Cope).

Those releases had reignited my interest in noisier guitar led stuff. As my Resonant label partner wasn't into that as much as I was, I decided to break away and do a label that was 100 per cent my own. Riot Season was born. The first release was a reissue of the seminal Japanese noise-rock masterpiece *Mellow Out* by Mainliner".

Why do you do it?

"Because I love music. I also love the fact I can put out music that I love (that sometimes maybe nobody else would) and get it to other people that may otherwise never hear it".

Have you ever made any money?

"Yes. But if you mean enough to make a good living out of it then clearly no. You can make money, and frankly for all the hours I put in doing everything myself I couldn't possibly do this if I had another full-time job as well. Well unless I was a hermit who never liked going out. The way I've found it over the years is this, first priority of any release once I've decided I love it enough to release it is to break even. It's a very difficult balancing act between doing what you love yourself and not throwing money down the drain.

I've released a lot of things that I've loved that have stiffed and proven impossible to sell. It's a total gamble really. Unless you go down this new-fangled 'funding' route where you will only go ahead with the release if it's fully funded in advance you are in the lap of the gods. If I press 500 records or CDs and they don't sell, the manufacturer still wants paying. So, it's only coming out of my bank account at the end of the day, nobody else is here to bail me out or pay the bills.

Over the years I've had to expand my original 'if I love something myself I'll release it' motto to 'I may love it myself, but can I really sell enough to make it work?' as there is only so much money you can lose before it's time to fold and admit defeat.

That's what happened to Chunky Records, the old mail order job. I got slowly and slowly more into debt with suppliers until I couldn't sleep or function properly. In that instance I got out of bed one morning, typed out an email explaining the state I'd got in to all my distributors and customers and ended it there and then. It then took me a good year or three to get rid of enough stock I'd still got to get my bank balance back into the black. Once you've had the VAT man knocking on your door at 9am wanting to make a list of things they can take against what you owe them you really don't want it to happen again, believe me.

Music-wise, I will listen to anything sent in, and once I find something I really love I must work out if I can release it without losing my arse in the process. Mini disasters do still happen of course, but they're a lot more minimal in damage than they used to be thankfully".

Your three favourite records, from the entire world?

"I can tell you one, AC/DC *Powerage*. That was the band that made me fall in love with music aged eight and that was the first LP I bought by them with my own money. That would be my favourite album of all time, and I can easily still stick it on once or twice a week and enjoy it as much as the first time. I can't pinpoint two others as there's so many to choose from, from all genres. I do listen to all types of music though, old and new and I'll never have any guilty pleasures."

In the group for this record was Rhys, Duncan, James, Bob, and myself. We recorded all the music in Dropout. It was a big departure for us, our three records so far were song based. We wrote songs, rehearsed the songs, played them live, then recorded them. For *Happy Birthday*, titled thusly due to us wanting to escape the negativity of both the previous record's title and as an attempt to usher in a new phase, we came in with no ideas. It was an exciting way to work. It was a lot of playing and a lot of editing. This happened both in post-production and during the sessions, picking bits that were sounding good and building on them. At the time we were into the German bands from the 1970s, Can, Neu!, Faust. A lot of bands began re-discovering them around this time. They came and went in terms of popular interest, I would guess that most people first heard of them when the Happy Mondays paid tribute to 'Halleluwah', with their tune 'Hallelujah'. Not that I picked up on the reference at the time, I was fifteen. As an aside I don't think the Happy Mondays get enough credit, they were a funky as hell band. Held down by the bass and drums, the guitars could shine. Shaun Ryder was a poet, he was a fountain for all that was going on in the UK at the time albeit somewhat enhanced by his intakes. Let's not forget, people love someone when they're going through the mill then will turn on them when the control is lost. Over-indulgence isn't as beautiful when you think of it as a cry for help instead of being an amusing character trait.

The album was made over several sessions, a lot of cups of tea and a lake of booze. Most of the vocals were recorded in the studio. James and Bob going at the mic with total vengeance hoping something would stick. I think James' vocal on the album's opener, 'War Crows', is one of the best vocal takes ever. The tune, to the untrained ear, is a two-note waltz time rager that disintegrates quickly, but he nailed it. It switches between two vague ideas with an oomph and then half way through the rhythm alters and things fall into place. If you catch a jam at the right time, if the recording facility is running, if the players aren't thinking but are totally in tune with each other, then you can catch something that is so satisfying. I'm probably the only person on the planet that thinks about this tune in the way that I do. The whole session for this record was recorded with the lights set to super dim. It was almost dark. I can hear the darkness. A few of the vocals were recorded in Bob's house, in his living room. Back in our previous band, Stanton, when we worked a lot on four-track we spent a lot of time in living rooms and bedrooms. You can tell a four-track recording as the vocals sound like they were done under a blanket. They are recorded quietly, so your family can't hear you, but then boosted in the mix so they distort. Check out any Sebadoh records from the late eighties, you can almost hear Lou Barlow's dad telling him his tea is ready. A couple of the tunes on *Happy Birthday* have this, only it's Bob's wife Becky telling him the dinner's done. If you find the time, and have the album, see if you can work out which hugely popular American rock band (seventies, eighties and into the nineties, and maybe even still) one of the song's lyrics were entirely lifted from.

The song 'Overlord Rapture in Vines Part 9', which we never called by its full title, using just 'Overlord', is another two-note jam. My fat string is tuned to D sharp and I play the string open and then the note two frets up. I'm normally tuned to C. I feel like a prog rock guitarist altering my tuning mid set, it's not clever at all. I had to do it because when I played it by fretting the second and fourth frets on the fat string it hurt too much. In fact, a couple of years ago I had to buy a new tuner as the classic Boss Tuner's digital display was too small and as I get older I'm thankfully seeing less. I switched to a Korg tuner, the letters are huge. The tune is fast and can go on for twenty minutes or can be done in three. Towards the end, following Rhys' drum cues we switch and hammer on the second fret at half the speed, making it one for the slower head nodders in the room. This tune is so simple, the drums do all the work. The pick-ups and drop downs alter everything. The vocal comes in on the drop-down bits then it switches up and the two notes get kicked into space by Rhys's brutal cymbal destruction. Bob did the vocals, but it can be chanted by whoever has a mic at the show. Over the years since the record, up to around 2015, we ended fifty per cent of our sets with this tune. It virtually always ended with us needing a hospital trip and if the nights gone well the whole room can be in a mentally destroyed state. There's a clear sense of relief when it finishes. No one wants another song, neither the band or anyone within three miles of the band. It's the ultimate full stop. Bob named it, and if I had to guess he looked at his record collection and saw a Pharaoh Overlord record, a Rapture record, and one by Australia's very own Nirvana rip off band, The Vines. Why not, eh?

We couldn't play all the songs from the album live. Or, more accurately, we couldn't capture the spirit of the recordings when we went back to them. We've never played 'War Crows' live which has always irked me. We could never do it justice, I have no idea why. Whatever magic juice we had during the five minutes we recorded it we never found again. It was probably down to the fact that James left the band soon after the release of the album; he joined Tim down in Worthing. They've spent the years since avoiding each other in the supermarket, not wanting their dirty secret to be made public. Absolutely understandable. Three of the songs became regulars in the set, 'Overload', 'Fire up the Tambourine', and for a while we played 'Tight Collar'.

We played all over the UK for this album, including a splendid little tour with Tractor who we ended up doing a split seven-inch single with a year or two later. We cover an Andre Williams tune, 'Jailbait'. By this point Tractor had been threatened by a band from forty years ago who had the same name, so they switched moniker to Field Boss. Anyhow, we toured with them and a chap called Wiz drove us in his red Transit. We hit up Leeds, Dundee and Edinburgh. There were fights at both Scottish dates, Leeds was calm in comparison. Dundee had netting above the stage. A week after the tour Wiz's van was on fire on a hard shoulder somewhere. It was on YouTube. I wasn't surprised. People film everything nowadays.

As you may notice, our tours are normally three or four days. The most we've ever done is nine. We are working people with families and these are Working Man tours, as we call them. We'd love to do four weeks or a couple of months through America but we're realistic and the choices have been made. We've learned over the years to pace ourselves. Who knows, maybe one day someone will offer something we can't refuse.

The art for *Happy Birthday* was done by Rhys and Tony Mountford. Tony played bass in Rhys' previous band, the Notorious Hi Fi Killers, and is a graphic designer. He's good at graphic design but not so good at reading Bob's writing, as the song 'War Crows' should have been called 'War Grows', which is what James sings all the way through the tune. I prefer 'War Crows' though, so all's well that ends well.

We contacted Andy at Riot Season, sending him the finished album. We asked if he'd be interested in releasing it. At the time Rhys was drumming in Shit and Shine. Back in 2007 Shit and Shine were a multi-drum affair, I think I saw at least 10 drummers at one show, I bet they did more than this. They were a very pummelling rhythmic affair with various noises over the top. They were a sight to behold. Craig Clouse the band leader ran his team with a strong arm and they were something that most folk had never experienced. He also played in the band Todd and Riot Season had just released a Todd record. Shit and Shine are still going, they are more stripped back, more electronic. The recent records are excellent. As I've said many times, and will never tire of saying, bands who don't change over their years of existence are bands that are lying to you. Bands shouldn't be giving you what you want, they should be dragging you around and challenging you. You don't need to like all they do, but you'll ultimately respect them a hell of a lot more. I am ninety per cent sure that Andy would have asked Craig if we were OK as people and OK as a band and I'm seventy-three per cent sure that Craig gave a thumbs up. This would have swung the deal. Most labels will do this. They'll like the music but if they don't know the people involved they'll have a quick and quiet ask around. It makes sense.

Here's a rule, and it's Ozzy Osbourne's rule as proclaimed at the tail end of *Decline Of The Western Civilization Part II: The Metal Years*. "Don't fuck with people on the way up as you'll meet them again on the way down". This rule, said by Ozzy's own mouth while pouring orange juice all over the counter as the film fades out (I will debunk this film clip later on, so if you're a debunking fan then stay tuned), is something to live by. Why fuck with people in your world? Why not be nice? Why not act like you're part of a team, all fighting the same cause? You're either Morrisey hating it when your friends become famous or you're in the squad supporting whoever's in bat. Craig must have said something nice, Andy released the album. Our first album to be released solely by someone who wasn't us and still, at the age we were at it, meant a great deal. Never get bored of being happy. Never get bored of being grateful when someone does something for you. Always remember. Cheers Craig. Cheers Andy.

Five Date European Tour, May 2018
Part B: Sunday May 27th

It's the morning. We're in a hotel. Three to one room, four to the other, refreshed after yesterday's big journey and show. Cologne tonight. It should take ninety minutes to drive. Touring Europe when the distances are short is the best. You get to see the towns and cities.

I make the executive decision to drive Mike Watt style. Him from the band The Minutemen has much tour advice to give and one of the things he says is to drive slow and conserve fuel. We have the time so I sat at fifty-five mph the entire way, riding in the slipstream of a lorry. On the off chance you don't know who The Minutemen are I utterly recommend you go and get yourself their double LP, *Double Nickels on the Dime.* It's an all over the place record that is born out of punk rock but goes almost nowhere near it, a genre skipper of an album. We drive straight to the venue. It is of course closed so we head into the city. Parking takes some time, and it is with great relief that we can lock almost all the doors on the van. Only the front passenger door remains unlocked. The van's electrics are collapsing. The windows work sporadically, the central locking system is FUBAR. There's only one keyhole and that's in the driver's door. I despair. It's at this point where I should rant about the modern world and how we rely so much on hidden mechanics. We're being run by machines. We stare at our phones. We have dishwashers. We are doing less and less. We order Tofu from Amazon. The broken down mechanics of the modern vehicle can only be deciphered by plugging a computer into the hidden USB port. 'Computers says van is broke down'. Cheers, mate. The mortal human can do nothing, we are done for. But I'm not a ranter. I will not rant.

Cologne, as is the case with all the cities we visit, is a friendly place with an enormous and spectacular cathedral. It could do with a clean but couldn't we all. When we have the time to see the town we're playing in it takes touring to a new and splendidly touristy level. We take in some sites and end up all sitting round a table, outside, eating. Pizzas and beers. Out of the seven of us, four aren't drinking. It's an age thing; we're all breaking slowly and realise we sadly can't do it anymore. I'm in my mid-forties, I need someone to plug a computer into my hidden USB port, I need to be told I'm broken down. Germany is the home of excellent alcohol free beer. We non-boozers join in and feel just as tough as the drinkers by having an ice cold Erdinger in a long and shapely glass. Which we don't steal. As tempting as it is. Anyone walking past would think we were a typical menacing British booze party. Where is your white garden furniture? Us English beer drinkers need to start launching it around your city centre.

The venue is on the outskirts of the city, it's called The Jungle Club and holds 200 people. Twenty-one people pay to get in. Along with the other band, Demon Head (from Copenhagen), and a few other stragglers both bands play to around thirty people in total. We were under no illusion, we'd never played Cologne before, it was a bank holiday weekend, we weren't expecting hundreds. Due to us setting the bar so low in our minds we ended up having an excellent night. The promoter, Sasch-Joe Bücker, was overly nice.

Too much food was supplied, endless drinks, there was a kettle and a coffee machine backstage. Demon Head, lovely characters, are on a four week tour playing a classic rock/black metal hybrid that intrigued. They're young and despite being into the final week of their tour they still seemed to be riddled with enthusiasm. Their English, as ever, put us to shame.

Weirdly Rhys recognised one of the guitars they were playing. It was a black Rickenbacker. It turned out it had belonged to a man called Gypsy who had played in a UK band called Querelle. Rhys' label, Noisestar, had released a record by Querelle. Gypsy had sold the guitar to a friend of ours called Laurence Price, who sang in Todd (as mentioned earlier, Craig from Shit and Shine's band). Laurence had then spent three years tour managing a Danish band called Ice Age. Demon Head are friends with Ice Age, so became friends with Laurence. Laurence lent the guitar to the Demon Head guitarist and there it was, on stage in Cologne. We are all one step away from knowing everyone. The world is a joke. There are no secrets. Everything is being filmed. Do nothing wrong, someone will find out.

We played a longer set, it was good to run through songs we hadn't played the night before. We went set-less, and it worked. No gaps, no big discussions, quick decisions. 'Hop the Railings' gets an airing, as does 'Experts Toll' and 'RRR'. Will has learned these songs well and is certainly giving the impression of enjoyment. The atmosphere amongst the seven of us is as free and easy as it's ever been. It's middle-aged wisdom, we've perfected it. Don't get stressed about 21 people paying to get in. They are there, they deserve everything you can give. If anything, question those that haven't come, don't take it out on those who are there. We come off the stage pouring with sweat having played as well as we can.

James left. We got Tim Farthing in. We also got Paul Sykes in. They joined around the same time in 2008. It was time for another revamp, it was time to have a frontman we could all hide behind, and Paul was the man. We liked his band, Men Of Unitus. They released one brutal album and played a bit in and around London. We asked Paul to join at Rocket Recording's 10th anniversary show in London. The whole of the London underground music community seemed to be there. It was a mild evening, we spent most of the time outside chatting and drinking and chatting and drinking. Around 10 bands played culminating in The Heads going on last, tearing the place apart. We were there, Paul was there, we asked him and didn't let go until he said yes. Tim was a Somerset person, finally someone to share the long journey's with. I'd played in a band with him in the mid-nineties called The Young Hurlants with Roo (Tim's brother) and Parrot on drums. Parrot's name is Nick Osborne, he now teaches music industry-related business in Hackney. He drummed in the eighties band The Becketts and the famous story of someone in the crowd counting 1-2-3-4 and Parrot cracking into whatever song was next is the stuff of legend down in the wild South West. The Young Hurlants played a lot in London. We were young and thought we needed a record deal. We stayed in waiting for the phone to ring for two years and then we stopped. Duncan also rejoined. We've lost track with Duncan, he comes and goes.

While I worked at Vital in 2001 postcards would appear sporadically. They were from Tim who was on an eighteen-month world tour as PJ Harvey's guitarist. 'At The Drive In are the greatest band in the world' said one. Postmarked Australia. He'd just played with them at The Big Day Out Festival, a festival that travels throughout the country. It was OK, Ladbroke Grove in the UK winter is just as nice as Melbourne or Sydney in the Australian summer. It was fine. I was OK. "Did you *want* that Baha Men single or *not?* No, I'm not crying, the line is fuzzy."

U2's lawyers have been in touch. I'm not allowed to tell the previously hinted at story. Ask Tim.

Thursday July 31st, 2008. Corsica Studios, London, with Acid Mothers Temple
First gig with Paul Sykes and Tim Farthing, plus Duncan Brown was back in the fold. We messed up a bit here and there. I spent the whole gig with my mouth full of snotty phlegm but seeing as I'm not really a punk or hard or a footballer I swallowed it. Nice place. Had a good chilli con vegan stuff. AMT played for two hours. Got home at 3.41am. Oh yeah, seeing as the car was parked in nice crime free Elephant and Castle we thought it'd be smart to leave the passenger side window fully open for a mere six hours. Nice to get some fresh air in the car. no one burgled anything though, I guess that's because we own nothing of worth. Oh for a proper job, with perks, and a sports club membership.

We don't pause when a new person, or new people in this case, join.

We had shows booked and we always have recording planned. Over the next month or so we rehearsed and recorded our side of a split twelve-inch with Dethscalator which Riot Season were going to release on their new side project label, Black Labs. Then straight out to Europe, twice in a week. First for two shows, one in Belgium and one in the Netherlands. Followed strangely by one in Berlin five days later. For some reason I go full Henry Rollins in the write up. What I fail to mention is the intense bleakness of Berlin Airport the morning after the show. It was early, we'd had two hours sleep. The waiting room was like a greenhouse, huge windows with the sun blazing in. The six of us green from the last 24 hours. The commuters looking at us like we were from the yet to be televised Walking Dead. We smelt bad. We looked terrible. If you're in an airport and see this sort of grouping of people don't make them move too fast and don't eat stringy bacon near them.

Friday September19th, 2008. La Zone, Liege, with Ultraphallus; and Saturday September 20th, ZXZW Festival, Tilburg, Holland
Killer weekend. Tim and I got down Dropout Thursday evening, hung about on the roof, threw a couple of beers down. Once all were present we loaded Jon's van and went to Paul's for the night. Paul and Dunc stayed up all night watching Laser Discs. Rhys wisely slept around the corner in his own house. I collapsed at 3.30. Bob tried to stay up and didn't. Left South London at 7am for the ferry. Couple of Stellas on the ferry. Got to Liege nice and early. Beers. Food. Beers. Great gig, Ultraphallus were nice chaps with a huge bass stack. Probably the best we've played in yonks, totally came together, although being shitfaced may have clouded my opinion somewhat. Stayed above the venue in a dorm style room. Had a cold shower. La Zone is a great venue,

all bands should play there when in Europe. In the van and onto Tilburg. The ZXZW festival is a week-long affair with a good mix of bands. We played in a venue called the 013, in the mid-sized room. Not sure we'll ever get treated in the same amazing fashion as we did for this gig. We had a dressing room. Oh yes. We got dressed in it. Well, we drank some beer in it. Watched Dethscalator who played in the Bat Cave room. We followed on straight away in the room beneath it. It was fun. Then from 6pm we had the evening to stroll around Tilburg. We get lost looking for The Enablers and Blurt venue. We sit around drinking with the Dethscalator chaps. As the evening drew on we checked out the Sun Ra Arkestra who pretty much blew our tiny minds. Then we end up sleeping at a guy called Mark's house. Leave. Van. Miss our ferry. Catch the next one. Back to Dropout. Home by 10pm. A top weekend.

Thursday September 25th, 2008. Cassiopeia, Berlin, with Pelican and Torche

Tim and I listened to Get In The Van on cassette in the car to get psyched up for this, so I AM HENRY FUCKIN' ROLLINS. Right. Wednesday night, it's dark, but then so is my mind, everyone should die. I'm up front with Tim, we get to Watford for 9.30pm. We don't stop. We drive all the way there and don't stop for anyone. This world makes me HATE. It makes me strong. Sleep at Bob's. Up at 3am to get to Luton airport. The flight is late. The English people, with their white trainers and shirts and caps and legs wide apart and shaved heads. Me: My arms are snakes, I'd like to kill every one of these knuckleheads. Look at them, drinking their beer at 5am. I don't need them. I have my shorts and my tattoos and my notebook. I have no friends apart from myself, and I don't like ME very much. Get to Berlin, Timm, our host, is waiting at the airport. He seems nice. Train. Tram. Bus. Get to his house. Bob and I hit the supermarket and buy food. (and beers, but I'm HENRY FUCKIN ROLLINS and don't drink. of course). Roll up to the venue, a nice-looking place, all graffiti and arty. The UK wouldn't allow this shit. It would get shut down, like MY MIND. WHICH IS STILL VERY DARK. HONEST. YOU WOULDN'T LIKE ME. The other bands come in. Look at these weaklings, so skinny I could snap them. Playing their weak music. John Lee Hooker would eat these fuckers for breakfast. I AM THE MOUNTAIN. I AM THE SEA. ha. That's for Bob. who likes WEAK MUSIC. We play. WE PLAY HARD. The day has been long, the other bands have been weak. This makes us play harder. Bob does 'THE GOBLIN'. Paul dangles from the ceiling and tries to strangle him with his legs. Duncan is KILLING IT. Rhys is BETTER THAN YOU. Tim is MORE FOCUSED THAN YOU. We do OK. Back to Timm's house for 3 hours sleep. Cab at 7am. Plane. Home by 3pm. THIS TOUR IS KILLING ME. I WILL MISS IT. I NEED TO BE KILLED. IT MAKES ME PLAY HARD. HARDER THAN YOU. I AM HENRY FUCKING ROLLINS. I WILL PRESENT A SHOW ABOUT MONSTER TRUCKS OR SOME SUCH WEAK SHIT ONE DAY.

We start working on our next record around this time, it's October 2009. We're in Dropout over the autumn and winter. As much as we were liking the freewheeling guitar freak outs, the go where you want for as long as you want vibe, we still liked the three-minute structured destroyer. Tim brought in the idea for 'Pope Long Haul III', we knocked it about briefly and it was done in seconds. We recorded it before we'd all learned it properly, but the essence is there. Since 2010 there's probably only been around five shows where we've not played this song. It's a very satisfying rock tune, the middle section can last a very long time as Rhys brings it up and down. Both Paul and Tim sing it.

I am not in any way anti-solo artists. I buy a lot of records and fifty per cent are probably by single people who have put in a lot of hours to create a solid work, like Tin Man, *ACID ACID ACID*, a four LP modern day lesson on mild manipulation of sound, Acid in spirit, hypnotic in feel; for the dance floor but also for our living room in BA16 – a solo artist of high and deserved repute. But, for me, when it comes to live music, it's very rare a solo person hunched over a laptop will move me emotionally. I've seen a lot. Most people who go to DIY shows have seen a lot. I get the cost factor, it's cheaper to be a solo artist, you can travel easier, you're a more attractive financial proposition for a promoter, you can create as much noise as a hundred people, you're almost certainly a decent person, and you're almost certainly doing it for the right reasons. But for me, as a dinosaur, when a band clicks and the electricity fires into the sky, when the whole unit turns on a sixpence and the swing changes, when the vocal hits on the one of a verse straight from the chorus, when the drums build it and the whole band drops in? For me, as a dinosaur, this is the pinnacle of live music. It's unbeatable. It still gets me. We have a few tunes that we must nail in terms of tightness. We have many that are more fluid but a song like 'Pope Long Haul III' is one that needs precision, even if it doesn't sound it – we can come across as being one big live fluke sometimes.

As a six-piece band, that we currently are, we have certainly not been offered shows due to the amount of people involved. It puts promoters off. Whenever I see a lumbering and unwieldy band with too many people my little heart skips a beat and I hope and pray they totally bring it live. The more people involved the more the band members must play with their ears. By this I mean you have to do a lot of listening. You need to find your place. You may think you can be a passenger but by doing that you become the weak link and there is absolutely no point in that. Why not be the best you can be with the resources and time you have?

When we were all standing and watching the Sun Ra Arkestra in Tilburg all our heads exploded. Watching a twenty-piece band performing at such a high level, *way* above anything we'll ever achieve, it has to be an inspiration. It's social inclusion, work hard and make it into the team. For the record, one of the best solo artists I've ever seen is Richard Dawson. Just himself and a guitar, he moved me. He also had a pop at the football shirt I was wearing, I think he thought it was a Sunderland top. Same for seeing the electronic artist Not Waving, playing in Shipley at a show we played at. He brought the ruckus all by himself. Or Bass Clef standing on the roof of the stage at Supernormal. Or The Rebel creating unease to the uninitiated, also at Supernormal. Or The Bug destroying my rib cage at Supersonic. Or Aphex Twin. Or Drmcnt. Or Danny Brown bringing the house down in Birmingham. Or Jlin making me dance in Bristol. Or Karen Gwyer, also in Shipley at The Kirkgate Centre. So, it's not *all* about bands, but often it is. I can't help it. Sorry solo artists, be as good as Richard Dawson. Aphex Twin, The Rebel. Bass Clef, The Bug, or Drmcnt, or Jlin, Danny Brown or Not Waving, or get a band.[*]

* Dear Editor, I may have proven my 'bands are the best' point to be wrong in this paragraph. Leave it in if you want me to look like a dick.

Saturday November 8th, 2008. 93 Feet East, London, Hokaben08 Fest with Otto Von Schirach, Acid Mothers Temple, Stearica, Chris Corsano and Mick Flower Duo, Aufgehoben, Dethscalator, Neptune, Team Brick, Zun Zun Egui, Vialka, Ramesses

Drove, picked up Tim, picked up Bob, got to Brick Lane spot on 3pm. Some delays while a load of hippies soundchecked. We played. Went OK. 93 Feet East is a funny gaff, onstage sound sucks balls but apparently it wasn't too bad for the people watching. Other bands who were good: Chris Corsano/Mick Flower, Neptune, Stearica. I missed things that were going on in the other rooms as I was on merch duty, although I did catch Birds Of Delay playing cards. Left a bit before midnight. Tim was bollocksed, he kept pulling that face Dylan Moran pulls in *Black Books* when he's pretending to be happy. Very funny. Then he fell asleep for three hours while I drove home. Nice.

Saturday November 15th, 2008. Jericho Tavern, Oxford, Audioscope Festival

Rhys:

The drive to Oxford is eventful. Paul overdid it the night before and is throwing up into his lap before we make get out of Camberwell. I leave him to wander up and down Woolworth Road for a bit while he sorts himself out and I roll one. Finally, we get to the venue which is a typical quaint Oxford family boozer. We load in past the young trendy's supping their gin and tonics and eating their pub lunches. The atmosphere is zero. There is no rock in this town. We have made a grave mistake. We load in, turn the volume up and play a good noisy set. We warm the room up but don't hang around. Back to London in time for Match of the Day.

Bob:

Duncan gets to my house, we have a tea. Wake up my daughter, drop her round to my sisters and have another tea. Jump in the car for Oxford, open the flask of tea we made for the trip. Arrive at venue, greeted by a smiling Paul and Rhys (They had no tea, but Paul was hungover). Load in the gear, grab a shandy and play a quick good loud set. I felt we should have been louder. Maybe 4pm is a little early for us. Load the gear out, pour another tea, head outta Oxford. Get lost, get to sisters, pick up the little one and home. Grab a beer. The whole Oxford experience was less than two hours, Because of this the official 100th Colossus gig will be back in Old London Town next week for the Plan B people.

Some shows like this Oxford affair, our supposed 100th show, do not rock. Playing in the daylight, straight after long drives, straight after work, straight after throwing up in your lap. They do not rock. Whereas somehow the Saturday before, also in the daytime, also straight after work and a long drive, rock did happen. There's no rhyme or reason. We can play exactly the same, it can work or not. These shows were in 2009 yet in 2017 we played a show in Ghent, Belgium, that was so disappointing for us that months later it still keeps me awake. The room was big, the show was well organized, we blew it. Yet again it was preceded by a massive drive from Somerset. What you're up against when you do this yourself is time. You have to spin all the plates. Family and work make up my dinner set. They all have to stay spinning and you've got to drive to Ghent and play. We were wiped out, we went on late, it was so disappointing. It was followed by a decent night's sleep in a hotel on the outskirts of town full of truckers, shifty looking single folk, cigarette burns in the sheets. The following night, in Lille we more than made up for it. It was Tim's last show with the band, not that we all knew it at the time. But we brought it in one of our favourite venues, La Malterie. People had travelled from Liege and beyond. We were ready and did everything within our power. This business is not war, it's love. You don't spray the audience and your band mates with fury, you bring it with empathy and the room will go with you. Even if your music is death metal brutal or grindcore or gangster rap, you bring it with the room in mind you can change people for the good.

'Pope Long Haul III' is a song that has a build two thirds of the way through. We sit on three notes (two really, as two of the three notes are C, an octave apart. This, in brackets, is for the musos and pedants. I hope you've ignored it if you have a life), for any amount of time, from a minute to five. It's up to Rhys. We await his roll to bring us back. The notes are the same notes as the chorus notes, just played way more muted. Again, for the musos, I believe it's called 'palm muted', where you play the notes, but your palm is deadening in the strings. It creates a chuggy sound. The decision as to when to bring the main chorus back in is, I believe, based on the room. The tension is key. The cyclical pattern of the notes is mildly frustrating as the big bit never comes. Everyone is waiting for it to come back in. The beauty of such moments is how everyone gets sucked in. We aren't the only band to perform such wizardry. A lot of our songs have moments that don't explode where one may think they should. This one does and it's a relief as much for us as it is for anyone watching. Also, after the opening riff we hit a hang note. For the bass it's the ninth fret on the second fattest string. We play the riff then go to that note and hold it, letting it drone out for as long as needed. Rhys will count in and the bass and drums play the verse. What you need to know at this point, as if you haven't already worked it out, is that I'm hopeless at music notation on the guitar. I know the open strings as I tune them to those letters (CADG is what I tune too). Beyond that and the further up the fretboard I go the less I know, aside from the 12th fret which I know to be the octave (the same note as the open string but in a higher pitch). Both the drone on the ninth fret and the build before the final chorus are examples of moments in our songs where we can fire off at a tangent. These parts keep it interesting as you never know what'll happen and we've all got to be aware of each other. It's the playing with your ears I mentioned earlier, you all get brought together in a moment of tension. It's beautiful, I recommend it to anyone.

Around this time we played a lot of real fun shows. We were promoting the split twelve-inch with Dethscalator, the split seven-inch with Tractor and the *Eurogrumble* record. It gets to the point where you can't work out whether you're releasing records and touring to promote them or promoting tours by releasing records. The key though was to keep busy and don't worry. Write songs that will be fun to play live and release as much as possible. We were on a roll, getting offered nice things and travelling.

Thursday November 27th, 2008. The Fly, London, with Ufomammut and Lento
This was a *Plan B* gig. *Plan B* is a magazine. Was, *OK*. Managed to get to Second Layer and All Ages beforehand, two splendid record shops. Played the gig, loaded out. Drove down Oxford Street to see the Christmas lights.

Tuesday December 1st, 2008. Windmill, London, with Todd and Dethscalator

Good night. Andy RS turned up with some little HC badges. We've never been on a badge before. Got home at 2.30am, got up two hours later. It feels better every time.

> *Rhys:*
> Good turn out and good sound. We do the usual shambolic stage show. Paul passes out, Bob does his guitar strap trick and I do my disappearing cymbal trick. Todd scares the pants off the remaining punters and we all roll home happy campers.

Friday April 24th, 2009. Opwijk, Belgium, with Zu and Kong (D-Tuned Fest II)

Was great. Picked up Tim in deepest Somerset at 7am, met the other losers at Maidstone services at 10.30. Beers on the ferry. Drove to Opwijk, few hold ups but got there easy. No sat nav needed for us, we use the force.. The venue is massive. Couldn't hear anything other than pure white noise for 45 minutes. Packed up. Watched ZU who were properly excellent. Back to the hotel. Bed at 4am. Home by 7pm. Brentford won the league today. A perfect 36 hours.

June 9th-June 13th, 2009. Iguana, Reading; Fred Zepplins, Cork; Richardson, Galway; Bunker, Belfast; Thomas House, Dublin

Zeroed the milometer and left Somerset at 12.30pm on Wednesday. Picked up Tim and drove to Reading. We had a rehearsal in Reading before the gig. It sounded terrible. Took just over an hour to find the venue that according to the AA was just under five minutes and 1.4 miles away from the rehearsal spot. The one-way system in Reading is ludicrous. The Iguana is above a fast- food outlet. The room is tiny with little or no soundproofing. There is a window, not double glazed, between us and the town of Reading. Silent Front were very good, they all took there tops off and played. I was wondering if they do this all the time or just because it was hot as hell. Not only was it hot as hell, it smelt. It smelt bad. The mixture of sweat and days old meat stench that greeted you at the top of the stairs in this place is not a concoction that I recommend you supping into your hooter. We played. Tim, Bob, and Paul shared one gaffered up microphone. This is not the first time our front three have shared such facilities, it tickles me every time. During the last 'number', our big hit 'Pope Long Haul III', the big windows were opened so the whole of Reading could lap up our joyful rock. As we reached our peak, as the orgasm of our sexmusic neared, Tim, a mostly gentle figure, one who is thoughtful and deep and all that shite, lost the plot. A three-second gallivant into the crowd. Guitar and all, pints knocked over. Then back, hiding behind his amp, head in hands, red faced. Very amusing and out of the blue.

We packed up. We shoved our crap into the van. We drove to Manchester. We got there at 4am. We had a couple of beers. We went to bed.

We got up at 7.30. Rhys' mum fed us up good and proper. Piling into the van we decided that we were going to not buy a map of Ireland and not get sat nav. We knew our way around. I'd been to Dublin once, twenty years earlier, that'll do. The ferry rolled a bit, but we held our breakfast down. In Dublin by 2pm. Easy. Found some not very good record shops and kept a close eye on the text to see if the Belfast date, originally set for the following day could be saved by the good people of Northern Ireland. It couldn't. Big shame. No idea what happened in Belfast with this date, maybe it'll all come out in the HC book. What a book it'll be. Anyhow. Wound up in a Dublin boozer, put some Guinness back. It was here our Ireland trip really began, a couple of soaked up young ladies decided we looked friendly and joined us at our table. The one who sat stroking Tim only had three sentences that she looped around for an hour. All of which ended in a cackle and a twitch. The barman spent the time trying to boot them out. It turns out drunk Irish ladies can call the bar staff of Dublin a 'cunt' or a 'fucking cunt' or a 'dick' or anything else and nothing will get them kicked out. Marvellous. It was fun. Turns out they were psych nurses pulling a sickie. We spent an hour looking for the venue, all was calm as we drove around Dublin. The venue was down some stairs in a black box. Met up with Them Martyrs, of whom Tebs is the guitarist who sorted these dates out for us. They piled out of their car all holding booze cans. It all boded well. A man was kicked out of the venue for spitting at the barman, he then got kicked out of a cab for being too drunk. I'd seen him getting kicked out of a different cab two hours earlier for being too drunk. I thought the English liked a drink. The American soundman, a lovely guy, took forever to set up three mics. It was baffling.

Consequently, soundcheck was cut to a brief one minute. Turns out this would be the only soundcheck of all the dates, but we're pros, we can handle it. Had the worst portion of chips I've ever eaten. Got halfway through and gave up. For 24 hours the oily potato chunks lolled in my guts. As I type this now, a week later, I still feel a touch bilious. They were horrific chips. Anyway. Played the gig, all went as smooth as things can. Made it back to Steo's house, Steo put the night on, Steo is straight edge, Steo owns a big sword, Steo is a fine gent. We slept on his floor, which doubled as his CD storage system. I think I slept on E through to G, Paul was H up to K. No one likes to sleep on Killdozer.

Got up, watched a Jesus Lizard DVD, then bowled out of Dublin. Due to Belfast being pulled we had a day off so headed to Galway to catch the first day of the Randal Records festival. Stopped halfway for a pizza and four four packs. Got to Galway, had a stroll round, wound up in a boozer, naturally. In fact, the pub owner took Paul's football due to its 'English nature'. It did have the three lions emblem all over it. Turns out the Irish really don't like England, or at least the England football team. But probably all of England as well; who can blame them. Doesn't stop them all supporting boring English Premier League sides though. Saw a couple of bands, Visceral Attack were the highlight of this day, and perhaps the highlight of all the days. Great straight up thrash attack, directly from the 1980s. They're all under 20 and totally slayed. Good mosh pit. Tim got kicked in the face. 'Bought' the Visceral Attack CD from the singer for a pint. Earache should put it out. Ended up back at a chap called Hicky's pad, staying up until 5am. Great night. Bob flipped out a bit, thinking his drink had been spiked, not quite remembering that he'd been drinking and smoking for 12 hours and being a bit shit faced is natural. He threw up and all was well.

Saturday morning. Up and at 'em by noonish, tucked into a fine eggs/shrooms/toast/beans breakfast. We headed in to Galway centre. Once the football was watched and Rob Green's whopping blunder was discussed to the bitter end we headed to the venue.

Watched a few bands (Them Martyrs and The Rites are the ones that spring to mind), set up and played. Was a pretty good show. Ending with a mini mosh and Paul getting hoisted in the air to perform some ceiling walking. A vastly drunk guy attempted to start a fight with us but couldn't string a sentence together and wobbled off. A few minutes later the police were picking him up for some alcohol fuelled misdemeanour in a shop around the corner. Ended up back at the house owned by The Rites' bassist and guitarist. Bed nice and early, around two, leaving Rhys and Paul to fend drug chat with the Martyrs drummer and his Bez-eyed mate. We're old and tired. But mainly old. Ho hum.

Sunday. Watched a Russ Meyers film, *Up*. Nice story about something or other. Headed off to have lunch at Supermac's, Galway's version of McDonalds. Met up with Them Martyrs and headed to Cork. The road to Cork from Galway is, for the most part, made up of pot holes with the occasional piece of solid tarmac. Rhys' three-hour dub step and grime mix tape helped us along. Tim, Bob and Paul really enjoyed it, sitting in the back, with my newly fitted speakers tearing their heads apart. Marvellous. Eventually arrived and met up with Eamonn who runs Rimbaud records. He helped release *Project:Death*. Later in the evening he was telling me about the misery of releasing a Serbian D-Beat Crust band's twelve-inch and still having 300 copies under his bed. Turns out Serbian D-Beat Crust doesn't sell too well outside of Serbia. Got to the venue, loaded in. Found out that although they had enough mics (well done!) they had no mic stands (not well done!). In an act of genius the mics we're draped over the beams in the room. They were gaffered on and left to dangle in front of the singer's gobs. As Bob said at the time, if Sunn0)))) had done this it would have been 'art', but because we did it we looked like tits. Oh well. Much hilarity ensued as Tim and Bob sang, the mics swung back and forth clocking them in the mouth, it looked like they were bobbing for apples. Gig was fine. Them Martyrs were at their best tonight, although they didn't think so. Back to Eamonn's, couple of cheeky cans of warm Carling, and a final night on the floor.

Final day, Monday - drive to Dublin from Cork, ferry to Holyhead, drive to Manchester, drive to Somerset. A long day. Ouch. Check milometer: 1230 miles. Total amount of time 'on stage' over the five days: two-and-a-half-hours. Bed at midnight, up for work at 5am. The glory. Cheers to Tebs, who's the calmest person we've met, for sorting it all. Cheers to Matthew in Reading, Steo in Dublin and Eamonn in Cork for sorting the shows in those towns. Cheers to The Rites duo for putting us up in Galway. As for Belfast, some other time maybe.

Saturday September 19th, 2009. Croft, Bristol, with Part Chimp and Tractor
Got to Bristol, via the Bookbarn, easy. It's always worth a rummage in the Bookbarn. Went on first. No idea whether it was any good. Got the Tractor split seven-inch which looked tasty. Drove Dunc to Temple Meads train station as he had a gig on the Fourth Plinth in London's Trafalgar Square. Back at Kunal's we drank till Bob was sick, as usual. 4am, on goes the computer to watch Dunc on the Plinth. Bed. 9am - Go get Dunc from Temple Meads train station, the boy looks like a zombie. The boy done good.

Sunday September 20th, 2009. Somewhere, Salford, with Part Chimp and Dethscalator

Scrape our carcasses out of Kunal's fine dwelling. Drive to Brum to meet up with Andy RS to pick up the Dethscalator splits. Get beaten at football by his nephew. Arrive in Salford around 6pm. Nice venue in the middle of a housing estate. Went on after Dethscalator. Got through it. Bob was sick post gig, naturally. Piled the gear into the van and Tim and I bailed before the Chimp played, unfortunately. Home at 2am. Up at 5am for work. A familiar tale.

Saturday November 7th, 2009. URA Gallery, Istanbul, with Part Chimp

The ultimate weekend of rock. Rehearsed Thursday night. Slept at Bob's in Watford to get to Luton airport at 5am Friday. Get picked up by Robbie, our man in the 'bul. Plush van into the city, us and the Chimp. Got fed some fine tucker at a posh restaurant, drunk, hung out, saw the sights. Saturday was more of the same but with added gig frolics. No idea how we played as there were four hundred beers waiting for us at the venue. By the time the Chimp played Paul was covered in margarine and Dunc was gooning one off behind Jonny C's drums. Bob was piggy backing Rhys across the stage, our host broke her neck and Robbie went home early due to "over-indulgence". Tim was continuing his "next beer tasting twice as good as the previous beer" theory with commendable gusto, Dunc lost his phone, and me? I was being a model citizen, of course. Next day we came home. The end.

And, of course, we played some terrible ones. Some shows you wonder why you say yes to them, it can break a human. Working, long drives, bad nights. You take the rough with the smooth. As I tell my kids: You must work to appreciate the times when you're just sitting around. The sitting around is no good if it's all you do. I also tell them to go to bed early and brush their teeth, but they do neither of those things. Maybe they'll just sit around all their lives. Do we listen to our parents? If I'd listened to mine I wouldn't have bunked a GCSE to get Faith No More's signatures. Look who's laughing now.

THE DRANG
from RRR
2011

When I moved to Somerset in 2007, I was jobless. I tried for Lidl as
it was opening nearby. Lidl turned me down. Then in November
2008 I became a postman. You may have noticed this from the
gig write ups, they are mainly me complaining about getting in at
3am to be up two hours later. BA4 is my postcode, there's around
30 of us that work out of the Shepton Mallet sorting office. We're
mainly a rural delivery office with solo drivers going out to the
villages. I'm often one of these, hitting up villages like Batcombe,
Ditcheat, Cranmore and Evercreech. All a few miles out of
Shepton. I don't mind the job at all. It's outside, it keeps me fit
(ish), and you get to meet all sorts of characters. The rural areas
of the UK are very neglected by the governments of this land. It's
like being in a Mad Max netherworld where you could leave a
body and it would go undiscovered for years. I'm yet to dump a
body but I have found lots of fields that act as decent and secret
toilet doubles. You get a sense of achievement when you go from
the 6am carnage of a room full of disorganised packets and letters,
to them being in the back of your van, to then around 2pm being
finished and back with an empty van. It's the only job I've had
where you get that feeling. Office jobs always have some work
leftover, something that can be put off until the next day. I also

found with office jobs that you could take it easy one day knowing you could make it up the next. That's not possible as a postman. The sorting office has to be empty at the end of the shift, it all has to have been delivered or delivery has to have been attempted. It's full on, the busy days can overwhelm when you first start. In fact, as I'm writing this, in March 2018, we've just experienced some ridiculously unseasonal Siberian inspired weather that some red top newspaper christened The Beast from the East. It's been brutally cold. The snow was so hefty that for two days we received no mail in the sorting office. This, on the one hand, is good as it means there's no work to do and you get the chance to complete any work in the office. When that's done, if you're lucky, you may get sent home early. The enormous downside to this is that the work is somewhere. It does eventually come, and as we knew would happen the following week was crushingly busy. It's one of those jobs that never stops, the work is like a river. The flow varies. The tide ebbs and flows, but it keeps coming and every now and then you get a crushing wave.

We have three songs that have taken inspiration from my time working in Shepton Mallet. There's a shop on the high street that gave us the title 'Dredges'. It's a hardware odds and sods shop called Dredge and Male. It has a picture of Bob Marley next to a fairy statue next to a camping seat on top of some paint pots in the window. An intriguing assortment. It's been there for years. The high street in this town, like many others, is currently suffering a downturn. The council allowed a Tesco to be built at the top of the hill and it's sucked the life away from the once busy main road. A great shame. This shop is run by a couple of chaps, similar age to myself. It's been handed down through the family. The fact it's somehow surviving is testament to humans need for both odds and, indeed, sods. It stands as a monument to stubbornness against the progress that is being assumed for us. For this reason we named one of our most harsh songs after it. You can find the tune on the *Eurogrumble* record, alongside the previously spoke of 'Pope Long Haul III'. I gave one of the shop owners a copy of the record, I am under no illusion that he listened to it. If you're after a copy of this record, which has been unavailable for years, go to Dredge and Male in BA4. There'll be one under the counter next to the Rizlas and batteries and desk fans and feather dusters and Christ knows what else.

The second HC song named after my time in the BA4 sorting office came about on the Valentine's Day of 2009. There seemed to be a large lack of any flowers or cards flowing through the building. It seemed the town was bereft of love this particular year. Shepton Mallet is the nearest town to the village of Pilton. Pilton is the home of the Glastonbury music festival. The festival is in the same postcode as Shepton Mallet and not in the same postcode of its namesake (which is BA6, in case you're interested). Yet the Glastonbury Festival is, obviously, not named after Shepton Mallet. There's a reason for that and it's not that Glastonbury is full of hippies and crystals and outfits made from hemp thus making it seemingly perfect for the festival. It's the lack of love in Shepton. Why name a festival after a town that doesn't tuck in on the Valentine spirit? On the split twelve-inch with the London noise rock band Dethscalator (who's output was this split twelve-inch and a record on Riot Season which I heartily recommend) we did a song called 'There ain't no Love in the Mallet'. The title of course pretty much stolen from the Bobby Bland song, which, by the way, is such a beautiful song. Making it almost the exact opposite of our noise splat. This record was a brutal piece of work.

As with the *Eurogrumble* record it's long gone now, only this time you can't go to Dredge and Male to steal their copy.

RRR, our fifth record, was recorded over a summer's weekend in 2010. We played on the Friday in Brixton at The Windmill. A venue famous for the dog on the roof and the regulars sitting and supping at the bar. They've sat through some murderous nights those regulars. Not being bothered by the grindcore in the corner, batting no eyelids to the laptop white noise all-dayers, nothing stops the supping. Fact: there is actually a windmill in Brixton. If you walk down the terraced street the venue is on, go past it and on into the park, it's right there. A windmill. In Brixton. We played, it was an all-nighter, bands playing for hours, we were on last, debauchery and carnage was everywhere. The regulars supped.

Saturday August 14th, 2010. The Windmill, Brixton, London
All-dayer.
400 or so bands playing. We get there at 9pm. Rainey Davenport, one of the promoters is shit-arsed, nagging us to go on, nagging us to go on, nagging, nagging, nagging. We eventually go on at midnight, by which point Rainey is asleep in what I assume is a pool of vomit somewhere. I thought Caretaker were a good band. A chaotic night all in all. We got away with it.

At the show were Jon Richards and Leon Marks, friends, comrades from other bands, all round good characters. Jon was in Rhys's other band, The Notorious Hi Fi Killers, and also Joeyfat (back from the Tenminutemen Peel session) and Unhome. Go find the Unhome record. Leon was in Headquarters, Shit and Shine and Sloath. He also drove a car around a field of cows a few pages back. We told them: 'See you tomorrow, we're recording a new record'.

They didn't show up at 11am so Rhys rang them. They hadn't believed us. An hour later they showed up and the first thing Jon and Leon did in HC was to set about recording a new record.

My memory of the recording of this record is much like everyone else's, I hope. A fuzzy blur, with brief, nightmarish, chill-riddled 'we've left the iron on' staring into the middle-distance moments. I remember the daylight of Saturday morning and I remember discussing with Andy at Riot Season about which formats to release the record on. Between these two events there's a few months' worth of memory utterly and completely missing. This was peak memory loss season for all of us. Since this time, we have for the most part, cleaned up our act. With the occasional slip. There's a song on the record called 'Warmer the Belter'. I recall the writing of this as it was only Tim and I in the room while everyone else was 'taking a break' upstairs. We took the chance to write a bass line and guitar part over the 10 minutes we were alone, and when the others came back down we played it to them and within 20 minutes the song was down. That's how the weekend went. 'The Drang' was no different, only with this tune we all wrote it at the same time. When you listen to it, it really sounds like it was written by eight people at the same time.

There's a lane in Evercreech, BA4, called The Drang. Before I had learned the Evercreech duty I knew the name of the lane.

In the sorting office at 6am all the postmen and women, bar a few, stand at the sorting frames. The letters and packets get sorted into their appropriately numbered pigeon holes and drop bags. The people doing the rounds will then come and collect the mail and packets so they can be sorted into the round's specific frames.

They can then be put in order of delivery into bags, trolleys or trays. The trolleys are for town rounds, the trays are for the rural vans. The Drang always stood out to me as being a most incredible name for a place. In our area we also have a lane called Kent, another one called Cats Ash and slightly less savoury one entitled Cumhill. The Drang always stood out so I looked it up and it turned out that a lot of UK villages have a lane with this name, it means a narrow lane or field between two roads. It's that simple.

Our 'The Drang' is five minutes of a bassline that loops in an ungainly fashion. It's locked into the drums with three guitars (Tim/Bob/Jon), a synth (Leon), some noise boxes (Duncan), and Paul's vocals sounding like they're cries from a cellar. The drums rise and fall, the guitars tear along. I can't put my finger on why I dig it. It may just be the song's title, who knows. There's so much going on. It's so very much not a traditional song, there's no easing in, no respite, no traditional chorus or verse, no easy way to find your way around it. The bassline drops out and hits the offbeat. The guitar line carries on like a three-man Viking rowing team. And then it stops. It was, like all the rest of *RRR,* recorded in a deep fug. It's probably just me but when I listen to this record, which I've had too recently as it's just been re-pressed, I can smell it.

Andy didn't want to release it on vinyl, he wanted it to be CD only. We thought differently. A compromise was reached and a very limited run of 250 LPs were pressed alongside the normal CD version. The main compromise was that we had to somehow sort our own sleeves. Normally the record label would sort the records and the sleeves, but there's a reasonable cost to both so we sorted the sleeves. We bought 250 blank gatefold sleeves from a German company and went to work on them. A local artist to me, called Sue Partridge, going under the name Chav, took on the enormous project of painting every single sleeve. We sprayed the outside yellow and had two stencils – the band and album title on the front in the same dagger design that was on the CD and the label logo for the rear. The inside of the gatefold was where Chav (Sue) went to work. Going through spray cans like the proverbial knife through hot butter, Chav spent three months painting and painting and painting.

I was being sent to the local car spares shop every day for more spray cans. After a couple of weeks of this I realised we were going to go over budget by way more than it would have been had we just made proper sleeves. I decided to write to the paint company. I explained what we were doing and how splendid it was going to be and that they should send us some free cans and we'd give them a credit and they'd look like they were supporting the arts. And all of that. They replied by sending three pallets of spray cans, around 300. I think both Sue and I both still have some left. I know I do as our youngest son got caught graffitiing with a few cans on a local wasteland area recently. A nice policeman called me during my standard Sunday afternoon snooze. I went to pick young Fredrik Thompson up.

The policeman said, "We'll see if the owner wants the boys to come back and paint over this, are they any good at painting?"

I took one look at their scrawl and daubings, "it doesn't look like it".

They got to spend a couple of hours after school in the police station on a 'don't do it again' course. The *RRR* sleeves looked incredible, everyone was different, and they sold out instantly. There was an art show dedicated to them in Bristol. Some of the records sold for a few hundred pounds. In early 2018 the vinyl was re-pressed with an extra record included that featured bonus material from the recording sessions and different versions of the songs. There was only one version of 'The Drang' though.

We played the song live a lot; it changed every single time. The beauty of having no structure is that there's no skeleton to keep the soft stuff in shape. It was a fluid beast. A beast with no bones.

Three weeks after the Windmill show. Three weeks after we recorded *RRR*. Three weeks after Jon and Leon joined, we played a show. The new line up's first show. I have no idea how we got a set together for it.

Saturday September 4th, 2010. The Old Blue Last, Shoreditch, London
Never been to this boozer before. Apparently, it's owned by the free magazine *Vice*. I slept for 90 golden minutes in the van before playing. I'd been up since forever. I'm sure Royal Mail are trying to kill me. We played as a seven-some, with added Jon and Leon. Got to say, it was very fun. The bands play upstairs while downstairs is a fine example of the worst pub ever. Full of gooning tits and crummy music, just like every other cruddy boozer up and down the country. This pub is a 'don't'. On the way home, during the times that Tim managed to be awake, we discovered that we'd both experienced the same *Fortean Times** experience while watching Rhys' drum sticks during the first couple of songs.

---

*   I've waited for this moment to elaborate on this *Fortean Times* happening. Yet as I sit here now on a snowy afternoon in the depths of Somerset I have no idea what happened. As Rhys played, it felt as if the whole world stopped and we were looking at everyone from the outside. Like we'd been taken away and dropped back. It was heavy.

We've got rough mixes of thirteen songs, we've sat on them for a month. We're listening back, working out what's needed. We're determined to not rush. The first fifteen years of this band has seen us release an album almost every year, alongside split releases with other bands, compilation tracks, seven-inch singles, and cassette releases. We've released a lot. The whole world can wait a little while for this new album. A new Hey Colossus record is not needed this year. We're planning on having at least one other long weekend in the studio. We'd like to get up 18 songs to choose from, to create the best 40-minute album we possibly can. Then it'll be overdubs, tidying up and editing.

At the same time this is happening we've been getting back into being as good a live band as we can. Tim, as mentioned, left last year and Leon has come in. We've had to juggle around what the three guitars do. Bob is now doing some of Tim's parts. Leon is doing some of Roo's parts. Roo has had to learn Tim's parts. Rhys and I have had to be as spot on as possible with the structures. You can't expect someone to learn new songs but then mess around with how the songs are played from show to show. You can do that when the line-up is solid. History tells me that's exactly what'll happen.

We've just had seventeen hours of rehearsals over three days. Two seven-hour sessions in London and a three-hour afternoon one in Bristol. After the Bristol rehearsal, on the 3rd March, we drove to Cardiff and Leon played his first show back in the band. Back in 2010 he joined for a couple of years but played the synth. This time, it's guitar duties. It's important to be in bands with people you know, people you have faith in, people you're friends with. At the level we work at there has to be an understanding that some shows will have thirty people in the crowd. There aren't vast sums of cash. Sometimes you have to drive home after a show even if it's 200 miles away. It's all worked around jobs and family. There's a trust.

The day of the Cardiff show was at the tail of the very cold and snowy period. It wasn't until the morning of the gig that we could say for sure if we could play it. A lot of events were cancelled around this time. We got lucky, though. The roads were clear of snow and with the added bonus of most other drivers wisely avoiding going out, they were also clear of cars. It ended up being the easiest of drives into Bristol for rehearsal and then onto Cardiff. The venue was The Full Moon. Last year the workers and locals saved this venue and have created a real nice haven in the centre of the city. The stage is small, but we cram on. The venue holds around 140 people and on Saturdays it's free entry. Despite the weather and the fact most people from outside of the city, including the promoter, don't make it, the night is a full house and a total joy. Leon's first show back passes without any problems. They even put us up in a hotel in Newport, 10 miles away. Cardiff definitely has hotels, I've stayed in one before. On this night for some reason we got sent to Newport. Not complaining at all, any warm bed is welcome.

The following weekend was Rocket Recordings 20th anniversary weekender in London. Ten years to the day since we asked/persuaded Paul to join. This was the show we'd been getting our chops in order for. We were on before Goat, Rocket's most successful band, downstairs at The Garage. This venue was a hangout from our youth; it was the regular spot for bands like Jesus Lizard and Guided By Voices to play. It was three stops on the tube from where we lived in those days. Then it shut. Then it was rebranded and reopened but I hadn't been back for 15 years. The night was sold out, 600 people. We played our nine strongest songs and had a splendid night. Rhys had the flu and had a handkerchief hanging out of his trousers all night for between song blows. We made a couple of mild mistakes, no one seemed to notice. The night passed without any issues. Paul was in the crowd towards the end like a flashback to Jesus Lizard's David Yow, appropriately enough. The merch table was buzzing. We sold our third highest amount ever. It's always excellent sitting at the merch table. Talking to people who have travelled a long way, finding out their stories. Sweden, Ireland, America, Italy, people had really travelled for this show. Rocket has a lot of love from around the world, people have really bought into their story. The Garage sounds better now than it used too. They've raised the roof and improved the overall sound. A lot of money has been spent. It is, of course, always under threat. The redevelopment of the area will never stop. The city will destroy everything.

We're not playing any new songs at any of the shows. Next week we're going out to Europe with our good friends Grey Hairs. They release records on Gringo and are a band who we love to watch. As tempting as it is to play the new songs we want to make sure they're perfect, we want to save them. When we've played songs from unreleased records in the past they end up on YouTube and often they're versions that don't end up sounding correct to us. Got no problem with people putting songs on YouTube. Most of our music is on there, via one source or another. But this time we're controlling it a bit by keeping the new songs under wraps. For the absolute record: we want our music to be heard by as many people as possible. We're all cavemen entertaining ourselves. The digital age is to be embraced.

While we work on the new record we're also playing as much as possible. After next week's Europe run we have festivals in Salford and Liverpool. At the end of May we have the Sumac dates in Belgium, Germany and the Netherlands.

It's funny to me, the thought that bands get things paid for. Not once in thirty years of making music has anyone ever offered to pay for recording, or given any tour support, or paid for the manufacture of T-Shirts, or paid for mastering of the record, or given us guitar strings or drum sticks, or offered to mend anything. But, along with thousands of other bands, a society under the main city has grown where you play the shows to pay for all your needs. You travel to places and sell your records and meet folk and build a network. Speaking for us, we do it out of both choice and necessity. We choose to do it. We do it because it's the thing we love doing. The fact that no one has ever offered to pay for any of these things hasn't stopped us; it shouldn't anyone. When it all comes together, and you record your music and work on it as a team having financed the whole thing yourself by playing and travelling and selling, you get a sense of pride. You've created it from nothing. You owe no one anything. The main difference between us now and us at the beginning is we're lucky that a label releases our music. They make it available on digital platforms I'm yet to look at, and they press our records and CDs, putting them into shops. As of March 2018, I'm unsure of sites like Spotify. We may look back at them as the worst thing ever. Or they could be the best. Ultimately, as said before, we want our music to reach as many folk as it can. The world is not what it was, but I know the underground will find a way before the above ground people get near to sniffing it out. It's always the way.

'RRR' from the album *RRR* is three notes.

Today is Good Friday, 2018. We got back from four shows in Europe at 9pm on Monday. I was up for work at 5am the following day and today is the first day off for what feels like weeks. I've eaten a full pack of Malted Milk biscuits. They were left over in the van. I love leftovers from the van. I go out to tidy it up and find full packs of biscuits and I feel like Charlie Bucket with his golden ticket. Then I eat them all. Then I feel a bit sick. But today is Good Friday and Easter's all about eating things that make you feel sick. I've always been very religious. Religion has always made me feel a bit sick.

The song 'RRR' has come and gone and come in our set. Currently it's a firm favourite. It moves like a free-spirited avant dancer. The version we're currently playing, the structure is roughly the same as the original. The bass is roughly the same but everything else slithers over the three notes like snakes might over prey. With a new line up, two guitarists who have never played it, it has taken on a new life. The beauty of having flexibility in your songs is the fact that no one is precious about precise playing. We like to know what we're doing, we like to not be on a leash. This song now has, through playing it many times, some quirks that a particularly average player such as myself could never be taught. The more we play it the more the freedom gets free. The more we play it the more it gets tighter. It's such a strange double happening.

This weekend just gone we travelled with another band, Grey Hairs. They're from Nottingham. We've known the people in this band for around twenty years. Chris Summerlin the guitarist was in bands I've already mentioned – Reynolds (from the Peel Session, where he'd had to change his trousers due to 'nerves'), Lords (where he'd had to change his trousers), Kogumaza (trousers), and now with Grey Hairs where all the chat was about trouser changing and struggling to deal with that area.

Touring with another band, a band of friends, and sort of being in charge of the organisation is like dropping a bag of skittles onto the floor from twenty feet and watching them dart about all over. Under couches, behind skirting boards, into the cat food bowl. Every service station stop is a military operation. Five minutes please, we've got a ferry to catch. The red skittle goes to get coffee, the green skittle heads to the toilet, blue hits up the magazines, yellow fancies a smoke but needs to borrow Rizlas from green so has to wait for green to come out the toilet. And on and on and on. It's all good though. There's twelve of us spread over two vans and we're like Dad's Army hacking our way into Europe. Making friends and attempting to be as nice as possible. Attempting to play as well as possible. Hoping people show up. Hoping to sell some records and T-Shirts to finance our service station stops. We stay in people's flats in cities we don't know; the trust shown is incredible. We flick through enormous record collections. We talk into the night. We thank them endlessly for putting us on, putting us up, and putting up with us.

We have just announced our fifteenth anniversary show. It's going to be at The Moth Club in London, we're pressing up a really limited live LP to have available on the night. We can't believe we're fifteen years deep. As I type this I'm dealing with the pressing plant. There's a fourteen-week wait for records to be pressed; the show is fourteen weeks today. It's going to be an old-style bootleg LP, like the sort us ancient people used to buy in the 1980s, before we could watch it all on YouTube. Back in the days when buying a live Pixies album with a terrible sleeve seemed like a very wise thing to do. It was the only way one could experience live Pixies in your living room. We'll see. Will they turn up on time? Will our plans fall into the river and flow to the sea?

Over the last six shows, in Cardiff and London then onto the four nights with Grey Hairs, we've played 'RRR' each time. It's developed. The guitars rise and rise in a way that I, the three note plucking bass player, can really enjoy listening too. Rhys and I have some stops and breakdowns that we perform. Once or twice I miss them but that's because I'm too busy listening to what everyone else is doing. Paul's vocals on this tune are perfect, four lines that repeat, four lines that give us all the cues we need to drop in and out. The fact this song came out of the tough to remember *RRR* sessions and has stood the test of time is very satisfactory. To be honest, when beginning this book, 'RRR' wasn't going to be included. It's snuck in through the back door.

I wonder if anyone thinks about this band as much as I do. I daren't ask. I sort of hope they don't, for their sake. I try and hide it, but I know I'm the one who nags. I'm the one who irritates everyone. One day I will apologise. I'm embarrassed to say that aside from my family nothing comes close. It could even be a problem. Some people are obsessive. I am 'some people'. It's been

15 years of emailing and phoning and rehearsing and chasing and tuning and playing and driving miles and miles. We aren't a big band, but we are a band that tries to develop, that has always moved onwards. It's the moving forward. It's the propulsion despite not now headlining Reading or touring America. It's the constant charge that I love. This song is an example of how we work. It's a combination of a rehearsal/writing process that other musicians would possibly despair at. It's an example of how we record, about how it's often the first take and no more. Catch the spirit, don't keep trying. If it's not there then it's not there, you won't find it by playing and playing and playing. I doubt any of us remember recording this song, but we've all grown into the song. It's snuck in the back door as it's back in the set. It's being played in a new and fresh way with miles of space and a spoonful of gentle heft.

We played Tunbridge Wells, Paris, Lyon and then Brussels. We then drove home. The weather was mild; it was nice to get out of the UK. It's *always* nice to get out of the UK. Grey Hairs had never been to France or Belgium. We felt like elders guiding young Jedi. Humans love it when they're guiding, we can't help it. Why is this? Why do we like the power? I feel ashamed to be like this. Tunbridge Wells was in the basement of a pub, capacity 50. We had decided from the off that all money made from the shows would be split fifty-fifty. In Tunbridge Wells we made £92.50 each. Nice and exact. The promoter was John Banfield, he ran Unlabel, a record label we'd all known for 20 years. They based most of their releases around the scene from their area. One year they released 52 albums, one a week. It was good to see John after a long time of no see. It was good he was still helping out bands. We stayed in a totally empty house 10 miles away from the venue. It had heating and water but not a stitch of furniture. We all almost got some sleep. Then we got up and drove to Dover and headed to Paris.

Two days prior to this a French TV company called Arte had been in touch. They wanted to film our Paris show and pick two tunes to put online. We said yes. They then sent a ten-page contract and asked us to digitally sign it. Of course, being ancient we had no idea how to do this so told them to bring a physical one on the night. We'll deal with it then. They did, and they recorded the set, and picked two songs. We've played Paris six times now and each time it gets a little better and each time more people show up. Every time we've played the city we've used the same promoters. We're firm believers in sticking with the same promoter. You can build a friendship, you work harder for each other. If it works and it gets bigger then everyone wins. If it doesn't get bigger you still have a friendship and will have a nice time. Our men in Paris are Victor Bournerias and Antoine Khoury. They've been there from the start. We love them. The show, for both us and Grey Hairs, was joyful. A lot of people came, we met some regular faces and met some new ones. You win towns over one person at a time. As we're fond of saying: word of mouth, we depend on it. After the show the 12 of us are split over Victor and Antoine's apartments. We listen to records and talk into the night.

For the first time we're playing the same set at every show. Having a newbie on guitar means we don't have the full set to pull from. We've learned around an hour of material. The real reason for only having an hour is that we've spent arguably more time on writing and recording new material than learning up old songs, but we've pulled it together. The set we have is: 'Honest to God', 'Back in the Room', 'Hop the Railings', 'Sisters and Brothers',

'Calenture Boy', 'Pope Long Haul III', 'RRR', 'Black and Gold' and 'Dead Eyes'. Arte, the French TV company, choose 'Sisters and Brothers' and 'Dead Eyes' for their website. We'd probably have picked 'RRR' as it's sounding so fluid, but I guess the crowd go more full-on for the upbeat numbers so it looks better on camera.

We'll have to learn up some more songs for the upcoming shows, we have to be excited to play. The fifteenth anniversary show, in fourteen weeks' time, is crying out for some new and fresh takes on old material. We'll see.

HOT GRAVE / OKTAVE DOKKTER

In 2012 Rhys moved to Japan. His drumming really helped my bassing. My bassing is decidedly average but because we'd been playing together as a unit for years I felt we'd locked in. His drumming is different to all other drummers I've ever played with. He's not a heavy drummer. From the beginning and up to around 2013-2014 we'd been considered a heavy band, but this was more down to the amount of us and the chaotic nature of our live shows. His drumming has more feeling than anyone else. He plays in a way that is so simple and with so much feeling. He told me once that he'd always wanted to play the drums and had done so from the single digit ages. He's never been bothered about what sort of kit he plays on, in fact as of 2018 he doesn't own a kit at all. He uses Roo's (HC guitar man, but also drummer in another band we do – Henry Blacker) spare kit. Roo had bought it when he was learning, then upgraded. When Roo hears Rhys play his spare kit he cannot believe how good he makes it sound.

There's a story about when Bad Brains, the DC Punk band from the very early 1980s, played a show that was being put on by Ian Mackaye and the Dischord people (the person and record label based in Washington DC, releasing music by bands from that area, righteous punks, major label rejecting, no drinking/

smoking, huge influencers). It goes along the lines of this: the show is set up; Bad Brains turn up with no gear. Ian Mackaye and all the other promoters panic and get a pile of terrible equipment in (their own stuff) and make 1000 apologies for it. Then Bad Brains play through it and totally destroy the room. Making no issues of inferior gear. It's all a myth. Bad workman blaming tools. You don't need the best, you need to be the best. As a comment on the way we live now in the twenty-first-century I think it says a lot. We love to spend money. We love to spend hours browsing the internet looking for new versions of things we have perfectly adequate versions of. We spend money; therefore, we exist.

Rhys's drumming was going to be missed when he moved to Japan.

From the age of 15 Bob and I had been travelling into London from our North London suburb to see bands. In 1989 it was heavy metal; Testament, Anthrax, Helloween, etc, etc. Then in 1990 we discovered a new world and began going more underground, seeing UK bands like Therapy?, Silverfish and a bluesy noise rock band called Penthouse. We'd travel up to see them at their own shows, plus whenever US bands came over the same UK bands would be supporting. It was quite inspiring to see. In 1991 when we went to Reading Festival and Silverfish played the main stage with Nirvana going on straight after them, it all seemed possible. We didn't realise it wasn't going to be possible as the goal posts would be moved, but in 1991 it absolutely seemed possible. In 2012 when Rhys moved to Japan and we needed a new drummer we got the Penthouse drummer in to replace him.

By this point we'd known Tim Cedar, the Penthouse drummer, for eight years. When we released our first record and played the session for Resonance FM back in 2004, it was this Tim that got in touch. From then we stayed in touch and with his new band, Part Chimp, we played a lot of shows and shared a split 10" record (with them, Todd and Lords), played throughout the UK and Europe and into Istanbul, and he'd recorded us many times in Dropout. Rhys suggested we ask Tim to replace him. So we did, and he said yes.

Tim's drumming is very different to Rhys'. All drummers are different so this is no slight on anyone. Tim's drumming is more thunderous, when he hits the kit the kit tries to run away. We'd known this from seeing Penthouse all those years ago.

Our last show with Rhys on drums, for now, was in Bristol, June 2011.

Sunday July 10th, 2011. The Louisiana, Bristol

A Sunday night in Bristol. I had ominous thoughts about such an affair. The Louisiana is a very splendid venue with good sound. It looks like it should be in New Orleans (see what they did there?) with its metal balcony and Southern states style look. Tim F and I got there first and loaded all the gear up the stairs, the others always hide around the corner till we've done it. Tim, Paul, and I popped to the Tobacco Factory to check out Chav's (the vinyl sleeve designer for RRR) art exhibition. The other two bands wore black and looked tough but seemed to play nu-metal or some poppy variation of metal. They will sell bucketloads. We don't wear only black and look far from tough and don't play nu-metal. We will not sell bucketloads. I think a band meeting is in order. Gig was decent actually, enough people showed up to make it a winner, the chaps putting it on (Burial Chamber) were diamonds, and I was home in fifty-five minutes. More gigs in the west country, please.

Our first three shows with Tim Cedar on drums followed.

16th-18th February 2012. London / Paris / Nantes,

Three shows with new drummer Mr. C in situ. London was with The Lowest Form and Liberez. Was a decent night. TLF: harDCore inspired grout, Chris Thrash bellowing away, belly full o' booze, over the top of grinding Void-esque riffing, it weren't bad either. Liberez, planking and plonking, straight outta Sarfend. The album they 'dropped' in 2011 made it into my top ten of the year. Yes: I make lists. I dug 'em, they had electronic drums and other zaniness I didn't understand. And a violin, which I did understand. Then we sprayed all over the evening, eight of us not all on the stage. Dunc was manning the bog corridor, Leon was in the side room chatting to the side room losers. Someone asked for "more" when we finished. We had no "more". Instead of telling him we had no "more" I was accidentally rude to him. Sorry. Back to Lewisham, Tim F smashed my bottle of red on the pavement, gutted. Downed some uri's and a kip on Mr. Paul Sykes' comfy sofa.

All up and at 'em early doors, meet up with Jon 'the best band driver in the country' Wood. We pile into his van. To the Euro Tunnel and onto Paris. The venue is decent, behind a restaurant. There is a decibel meter – we're not allowed to go above one decibel. We get fed. We get watered. Victor, our host for the evening is a gent. He looks like he should be shuffling around in an arty black-and -white Euro film, smoking and mumbling. We play. All is good. Back at Victor's house, armed with a crate of Euro-fizz and some wine we drink the night away and eat Victor's 'pasta special' which is pasta. And nothing else. No complaints of course, but we did have a rummage around his kitchen for something to make the pasta special be a bit more special.

Nantes, a three to four-hour drive from Paris. One of those nights that lives in the memory. Or would of if they hadn't of had a free supply of red wine dripping into our stupid English guts all night long. We went for a pre-match walk with Mr K.F.Whitman, who seemed utterly at ease, despite being out-numbered eight-to-one. We saw a massive mechanic elephant. The venue is in a disused big building. Upon arrival we were informed we were to go on last, after all the 'big' names, after (we assumed) everyone had gone home. A man played some boxes while a woman made noises with her lips. Some 8mm films of solid black squares played while some quiet drones tinkled away. Peter Brotzmann and a couple of pals tore it up. KFW performed his quadrophonic synthscape that was very excellent. Then we set up, no soundcheck, and did what we could with what we had at our disposal. And it went well. People stayed to watch, and no one audibly booed. We got away with it. We celebrated by tucking into free booze. We got paid some cash and spent it all on the record stalls that were set up there. We slept in the building. We were awoken by a man who either wanted to fight or screw us but luckily he fell asleep on the floor before either happened. Jon 'the best band driver in the country' Wood drove us home. No one had embarrassed themselves, no one had lost anything. It was a killer three date working man's tour.

We went in to Dropout to record *Cuckoo Live Life Like Cuckoo* in 2012. The recording session wasn't too dissimilar to the *RRR* sessions only this time we were more determined to capture exactly where we were at. Maybe. Who knows. I'd gone in with two ideas, Bob had one, Jon had a couple. It was going to be another fluid session where we wouldn't know what was to come.

Leon had set up six synths over two tables, Duncan was bunkered down in a corner surrounded by his pedals and magic boxes as was Paul, who on the recordings was working the electronics. He planned to add his vocals after. Tim C on the drums and setting up the studio for the session. Wires were everywhere, there were too many of us in the room. It was a perfect setting.

'Hot Grave' began life as a couple of bleeps on a Nintendo Gameboy. Like humans beginning as a single cell and growing into the disaster that we are now, this song had very humble beginnings. Jon plugged his little handheld game machine into the PA and the bleepy rhythm started. Once we'd decided on the two notes that we were going to play all the way through (Open C and three frets up) we began working on the groove. Tim C was very keen on dynamics, so we had a lot of ups and downs throughout the six minutes and forty-five seconds. It starts with Jon strumming one chord and Leon working some synths, Tim cracks three snares and we're all in. Tim F is playing the lead line, Jon stays on the single chord (adding another later on), Bob and I play the two notes, Duncan and Paul are buried up and over with their sounds. The drums drop in and out and natural builds began happening. It was a jam with a vague plan. Jon added some guitar overdubs with us all in the control room watching. It all came together beautifully.

Then we had a two-note jam recorded. With no vocals. It lasted six minutes and forty-five seconds and to be honest it wasn't all that.

We went home. The mixes were sent around, and I don't think I was the only one who dismissed it as a hopeless and aimless jam that was destined for the reject pile. The playing was good, but it went nowhere.

At the next session Tim F said he had worked on some vocal ideas for the tune and that it was going to be called 'Hot Grave' and can someone please press the record button.

Watching Tim F do vocals is akin to watching Brian Blessed bark a booze order across a rammed Soho drinking den while holding forth on all manner of subjects surrounded by a table of luvvies. He gives it all. A sight I will hold with me. The words and the manner which they are delivered on this tune utterly make the tune. It became a noose round his neck as the years passed. People would ask for it and it stuck out like a sore thumb in a set of tunes that had somewhat moved away from 'Hot Grave's' feel. But we all liked playing it so at the end of a set we could reel it out with confidence. The song arguably became our calling card for a year or two. It was in *The Quietus'* top ten 'Writer's Tracks of 2013', it would get characters moving. Two notes, taken from a Nintendo Gameboy, turned into a throbbing head nodder with a lesson in lyrical delivery that shredded vocal chords.

Round this time my dad moved to Somerset. He'd roamed about a bit and ended up down in the South West. Picking our town purely because we live here. His garage has become our gear storage area. He fixes our broken speakers and loves going to Screwfix to pick up replacement caster wheels for our decrepit amps and speaker cabinets. He's the man you see walking around your town. Every town has three or four men who stroll around. He's one of our strollers. Since owning a strolling father I've noticed many such men in many towns. I think it's what happens to men who work all their lives outside and then retire. They start strolling because they cannot work out what they're supposed to do with all the energy they used to use up when working. They're coiled springs. If you see a stroller lead him to your garden and your unmade shed, it'll be up in a day. It'll only cost you 3000 cups of black coffee (the ideal outdoor working drink, apparently. It stays warm for a decent amount of time due to lack of cooling milk. It can be drunk almost cold unlike tea which has gone wrong way before its temperature dips).

Each evening he comes around and drinks our tea. He doesn't have milk at home as it doesn't sit comfortably in him, or something like that. So he comes around and drinks ours. He got to grade eight at piano and was, for a brief while, in Rick Wakeman's band at school. He was the band's trumpet player, there was a decent enough pianist involved already. They were called The Manor House Five. Rick's cousin Alan was also in the band, he played the clarinet and ended up in Soft Machine. Rick was the year beneath dad, Alan was in the same year. Their art teacher joined on the trombone; it was Mike Westbrook, a leader in the avant-jazz world scoring up all sorts of Wikipedia-entry-worthwhile experiences. I like to believe it, true or not. What is true, and I had it confirmed when I Tweeted Wakeman, is that dad made the future cape-wearing prog pusher's first bike. Cycling is my dad's first love. I think it goes: cycling, strolling, Brentford FC, coffee. That order. So, while the Wakemans and Westbrook were perfecting their music chops dad was racing around West London on his bike. Rick Wakeman was a Brentford supporter at school then switched to Manchester City. They went to school in West London. If you're the sort of person who switches teams you'd better have a damn good reason. I will ask him, one day, probably via Twitter.

When *Cuckoo* was in its rough mix stage dad would come over and demand to listen to a couple of tunes. Namely 'How to Tell the Time with Jesus' and 'Hot Grave'. Both are made up of one riff all the way through. It'll be an abiding memory for me seeing him with my £9.99 Sainsbury's headphones on, eyes shut, smiling like hell. The songs seem basic and complicated at the same time. I guess they hypnotise strollers. Maybe they sound like a factory clanking away, so provide comfort.

He didn't like them so much once they were mixed properly. The sound did change. They were more metallic and industrial before, they (you may be surprised to hear if you know the songs) are way smoother in their finished state. If you've ever watched Lars Ulrich getting advice from his dad in the Metallica film, and I heartily recommend you put this down and go and watch that film right now, then you'll have a rough idea how it went down in my kitchen in 2013.

Cuckoo was released by MIE Records. Henry Tadros ran MIE and his label was more on the leftfield experimental tip than what we were peddling. I loved his label then and still buy records he releases to this day. If you want to check out what he releases I recommend the Pelt record and the album by Gate. Both on the droney scale but put together with a certain panache that take them above and beyond. It was a surprise to a few people when MIE released our record, but not to me. I run the mail order department for HC (the mail order department for HC is boxes of records and T-Shirts in the garage and two sites where we sell from, Bandcamp and BigCartel. That's it. When orders come through either dad, Stan, Elisa, Freddie or I post them. Sometimes with a note, sometimes with a free record, sometimes with nothing, but always with love). I pay close attention to who orders things. Henry ordered records and T-Shirts from us, and this information was spotted and filed away for a future day. *Cuckoo* was the future day. We sent him the finished record and he dug it and that was that. He pressed 500 LPs and the same amount of CDs. The vinyl has since been re-pressed with a hot as hell 3D sleeve with some old skool 3D glasses included. I have a great Cramps record where they do the same thing. The artwork was drawn by Tim F, it's a cuckoo smoking something that makes him and us see octopi float off into the sky.

During the *Cuckoo* sessions some ideas were brought in. Bob brought the riff to 'Leather Lake' which we recorded and could never play live. No amount of practice could make it tick. We have a fair few songs like that right up to this day, they record well but are unplayable live. It was the same for 'English Flesh', another tune from *Cuckoo* that Tim performed his Brian Blessed vocal for. It was about piling racists up and burning them in a whopping bonfire. Despite the perfect sentiment we could not play it live. The recording was perfect, we just never matched it. It was the downside of recording jams and editing. It was frustrating at times.

One of the basslines I brought in was for a tune that ended up being called 'Oktave Dokkter'.

I walk up to ten miles a day at work, I like it. Unless it's pouring. I don't like it much then. Although even on those days I love it when I get in and think to myself that I've been out and exercised on a day I wouldn't normally have. I get a good amount of time to think and plot and scheme and come up with new thoughts. Most are crazy, as Elisa can testify. "No, we're not moving to the new flats they're going to build on the soon to be demolished Griffin Park". And, "No, we're not going to buy a Mercedes Sprinter just for band stuff". She didn't mind when it was suggested I have a vasectomy, that idea was OK apparently. It was even arranged to happen on Valentine's day, 2014. Pure love. *Anyhow.*

One of the things I do to pass time while out on delivery is write basslines. I do this by clacking my teeth together in rhythm while humming the notes in my head. It's a habit I've picked up from somewhere, no idea where. One day my dentist, a particularly tough but fair Romanian lady, will wonder what the hell has happened to my flattened nashers. I will lie to her. Also, as an aside, and this seems like the correct place to mention it; I play the bass in my sleep. Elisa's arm is the fretboard. I don't think she's really into it and the bruises can look suspicious, but no one asked her to marry me. Well, I did. But no one made her say yes.

This is how the tune that became 'Oktave Dokkter' came about. The bassline was longer but in the spirit of equal rights and fair play it got stripped back to make it a little simpler. Bands can do this, destroy your hopes and dreams of playing a ridiculously over complicated bass line. Bastards. Of course, it made total sense. You need others to tell you you're being a fool on occasion. The song starts with the drums and bass. The drums are playing a Queen-esque 'We will Rock You' rhythm while the bass line syncopates against it in a manner that is vaguely uncomfortable. Over the course of the whole song the bass doesn't alter at all. It loops the riff, only getting louder. Everything else swings and swaggers against it. The guitars play gentle folky lines then stop entirely and come back in and stop and come back in. The vocals come in and leave. The tune picks up and by the end everything is set to destruction. The drums straighten out a little and for a minute or so it's the slightly uncomfortable riff played by all in a loud fashion. Then, as most bands who base their tunes around loose structures will do, there's a few key moments that signal the end is nigh. In this case it's when the drums go down to the toms (no cymbals, just the actual drums) that we all know the song is four loops* of the riff from the end. Then we stop. When I talk about music with my sons I tell them it doesn't matter what happens, if you all stop at the same time at least it looks like you know what you're doing. Pulling the wool over people's eyes for, at this stage, in 2013, ten years.

Over the last five years this is another tune that has morphed and is arguably tighter now than when we recorded it. We all know what we're doing. Cedar was the drummer on the recording, but Rhys came back in 2014 and the song changed slightly, the heavy drums were swapped for more feeling. Again, all drummers are different, both Tim and Rhys are great drummers. It's horses for courses. We played the Supernomal Festival in 2012, Tim's drums were running away from him. They seemed terrified. After he said it was just like being back with Penthouse, chasing drums around the stage, hooking his legs around things to keep them from moving. We recently played with a band (La Pince, from Belgium and France) who's drummer had the same issues. He'd resolved the problem by tying bungee ropes around his kit. It

---

* I know it's Tim Cedar drumming on this tune but when Rhys reappears in a little while this little paragraph is relevant. Rhys hates it when the stringed instrument people talk in numbers. We're going to play the riff round four times then do that bit eight times, etc. It turns out we all count things in different ways and from different points. My eight could be his 16 could be Bob's four. Also, it's about the feeling with drummers. They're not playing the riff. They don't care about the riff. They care about the feeling. I'm beginning to understand this, thirty years into playing music. Drummers don't play riffs. Got it. Leave me alone to count loops, clatter my teeth to the rhythm and hum along.

seemed to work, I made a note. It could come in handy one day.

When it goes off at the end of 'Oktave', and we're all in harmony, it's so very satisfying. What's also very joyful about this song is when Rhys and I start there's no count in. We look at each other and come in together. I think because the first note hangs a little I can hear the second beat arrive so get the timing quickly. We always start it as the previous song is fading out, we don't need to wait for everyone to be in tune. They can fiddle while we're playing. You need a song or two in the set that can crack in without the need to check whether everyone's ready to go. No messing about. Not only is the song on *Cuckoo* it's also on a limited edition of one copy lathe cut seven-inch which is owned by someone in Manchester. It was a present from her friend. We were asked if it was OK and being utter vinyl nerds, we naturally said yes. If you think you have everything we've released, chances are, unless you're the woman in question, you do not. Sorry.

16

Five date European tour, May 2018
PART C: Monday May 28th

It is 7.56am on the morning of the 28th. We've been awake for what feels like hours. The hotel has no curtains and the sun is streaming in. Our room hangs over a dual carriageway that has been alive with lorries and sirens and speeding cars and shouting since 5am. You forget what day it is. We're only doing five days but by day three the transition is complete and you're in tour mode. Last night was a Sunday. No one goes to shows on a Sunday. Today is Monday, the traffic is rush hour related. We're going to be heading to the town of Kortrijk in Belgium to meet up with Sumac again. They were elsewhere last night at another show in another city. Like Sundays, Mondays also carry with them the tradition of ill-attended shows. We shall see.

Rhys is covered in mosquito bites, he is the only one of us with them. It's been hot and humid, the mosquitos came out to feast on Rhys. We swing by a pharmacy on the way out of Cologne. It's an easy drive to Kortrijk, three hours. Another day of Mike Watt driving is in order. This is also day three of a miraculous run of hotels. This is abnormal. We keep telling new guy Will to not get used to it. We head straight to the accommodation, book in, get into our rooms and feel excellent. It's honestly something that is way above and beyond any of our dreams, it's so damn exciting. The venue is a two-minute walk away. Across from the hotel there is a poster for the show.

Top tip for promoters: If you want the band to be impressed by your promoting, put a poster for the show on a wall opposite their accommodation.

The venue holds 550 people, it's similar to the place we played in Nijmegen in that it's in the centre of town and next to the train station. The venue has a back stage area to die for. It has a roof top terrace, shower, kettle, fridge full of liquids, a fine spread of cheeses, crisps, peanut M&Ms and a kitchen area with joyous smells pouring out.

Sumac soundcheck while we admire the wall of Polaroids showing all the previous bands that have played there, including Skid Row, Dog Eat Dog and Udo.

We soundcheck, then eat, then play.

The show is good for us, we have thirty minutes and we're on at 8.30. We pick a mixture of songs, we go 'Honest to God', 'Back in the Room', 'March of the Headaches', 'Sister and Brothers', 'Pope', 'RRR', 'Dead Eyes'. Half an hour of pure entertainment and we're off, pouring with sweat. Gear off the stage and straight into the van which is parked right next to the loading bay by 21.07. Job done.

Sumac play and crush the hell out of everyone. I'm enjoying the playing within the band, Aaron is channelling some Keijo Haino while Joe is tuned so low that the fat strings are flapping, making our trousers swing. Nick Yacyshyn the drummer is weirdly providing the melody, or so it seems.

It was a well-attended show. Being the support band on these little tours is both tough as you're not playing to people who have come to see you, but enjoyable for the same reason. It's a challenge. It forces you to not be lazy. You aren't preaching to the converted. Blank faces can stare back, the end of a song can be greeted by muted response. It's good for you, it makes you learn about your music.

By 11.30 we're back in the hotel and soon asleep. I love it.

WITCHFINDER GENERAL HOSPITAL
twelve-inch
2012

17

I know it's hard out there for a dinosaur,
What do you collect all those rare vinyls for?
  –Open Mike Eagle, from his tune 'Your Back Pack Past'

Our releases need to be on vinyl, or CD, or cassette. Digital releases are thin air, they can't be grappled with, can't be hugged. Can you hold a download close to your heart? Can you obsess for years over the artwork of an iTunes purchase? The grotty crackle of a record, shouting its age at you as you spin it for the 100th time, it's part of your life. A record you've owned for the majority of your existence, wear and tear for all to see, telling your stories with a bent corner or a wine spill stain. It's entwined within you, it's wrapped around your gizzards. As a band we're all the same. We spend more time hunting out record shops in towns we're about to play in than any other tourist attraction. We are vinyl nerds. Sometimes it feels like it's the reason we've travelled across Europe. Recently spending two hours in a record shop in Ghent prior to a show, as opposed to looking at anything else that fine city has to offer, proves this. There's a chap who turns up to 80 per cent of our North East France/North West Belgian shows with a large box of records. He sets up next to our merch. We all drop euros on his wares. He knows this. He's our dealer, pushing his drugs on us.

Today's post included the second solo album from Moe Tucker. The drummer from the Velvet Underground released some marvellous records through the 1980s and into the 1990s. People listened to Underground Lou as he went on, people forgot Underground Moe. They shouldn't have. I couldn't wait for an original copy of the SS Decontrol debut, currently at around £700 on Discogs, so I've picked up a decent bootleg. I'm not proud. I needed some early eighties Boston straight edge in my life, we all need some early eighties Boston straight edge in our lives. So bootleg it had to be. The third and final record in today's post was the Spazz 2 LP compilation, *Sweatin' to the Oldies*. Who's still listening to Power Violence influenced hardcore late on in the 20 teens? Killer compilation on clear vinyl, comprising of the band's long out of print singles and compilation tracks from 1993-96. Meanwhile I'm waiting on Donald Byrd's *Places and Spaces* LP, from the mid 1970s on Blue Note. I've picked it up from an Alaskan DJ who's clearing his record collection. Who said the internet is bad?

I am a vinyl hoover. I sweep up your unwanted records. You can grow up if you want. You can clear some space in your living room if you want. You can do what you want, if you want. I'll have your records though, much appreciated.

A request. Vinyl doesn't fit through your letter box, as many packets don't. Speaking as a postman may I request you create a spot somewhere around your house where the plucky post person can leave your oversized parcels? A secret spot. Somewhere safe. Yours, all post people from around the entire world.

Sometimes we release records that are irritatingly limited.

The following chapter is about such a release. It was only two songs, two long songs. We're vinyl dinosaurs, we've always bought records, we love physical releases, you've got this fact now. Onwards.

This record is such an excellent example of why I am fully into the idea and reality of the underground music world. It's a twelve-inch released by a label called OneC based in Plymouth. They got in touch, 'they' being Pete and Kathryn Davies. The initial conversation went like this (if you want to know how huge deals go down in the music industry look away now):

Hi Joe,

This is Pete from One C based down in Plymouth, we've been putting records out since 2008 and are just about to release our 22nd one, amongst these have been a series of lathe cuts which I have now resurrected again after I found someone capable of doing them to a high standard. Would you be interested in putting out an 8" lathe? obviously a Hey Colossus one would be grand but if this is not possible then any of your other projects would be good. It would be limited to 50 only. We just had one done by the new guy and the quality is very good, they do not knacker your needles nor do they degrade after multiple plays. Pic attached. If you need any more info etc just let me know,

Cheers,

Pete

Pete,

Cooooooool....I'd say HC would definitely be up for this if that was OK? What would you need from us? in terms of length of music etc...We're overdubbing stuff on Sunday for a new

album, so you could get it sooner than you want...ha...! Cheers
for getting in touch, lemme know details, take it easy

Joe

Joe,
Oh yeah be really happy if HC can do it! Finally managed to
see youse at the Croft with Harvey Milk the other month, and
I'm off to Supernormal for more! Maximum we can go to is 9
mins per side on the 8". just need the music as wavs which I'll
get over to the cutting guy and then we're off! Artwork can be
whatever you want, I can do screen printed sleeves for example.
Cool am happy to have the music sooner!!

Cheers,
Pete

Harvey milk was chaos...Supernormal will probably be as well!
Make sure you say hi, I'm bassman! OK, we're on the case with
it. something will wing your way....Nice one!

Joe

That was it, the song length was discussed. We sent them
'Witchfinder General Hospital' for the A side, it was 15 minutes
long. For the B side we sent them 'The Butcher', clocking in at
a mere nine minutes. A twelve-inch was pressed up on normal
vinyl (not lathe cut). Tim F did the art, it was a Witchfinder with
a head that could be looked at upside down or the right way up.
OneC screen printed them, they all sold in about 24 hours, and
that was that.

In case you're not an adenoidal music nerd let me quickly
explain what a lathe cut is. For although we didn't end up doing

one for this release they are intriguing things. They're most famously produced by a chap based in New Zealand called Peter King. Over the recent years they have spread and now most countries have at least one or two people making them in their sheds and bedrooms. You need a lathe cut machine, you need some sound skills and you need a ton of patience for they're created one at a time in real time. If the record is 20 minutes long it takes 20 minutes to make one lathe cut. They look like records, they have the same grooves and printed label and they're, more often than not, the same size and shape as a record. The difference being they are made from a slightly different material, they are thicker than flexi discs (the thin plastic 'records' that were often given away in the 1970s and 1980s on cereal boxes and the front of music magazines) and traditionally slightly thinner than normal records. They are also more fragile and instead of the black of a record they are normally clear in colour.

At this point I thought I should quickly speak with someone who makes lathe cuts. Phil Facy, who runs 3.45rpm Vinyl Lathe Cutting down on the South Coast. He says, "I cut in both clear and black, and use three different thicknesses (1 mm / 1.5mm / 2mm), they are as long lasting as normal vinyl." He spends days upon days cutting records in various quantities for all the underground labels throughout the world.

The benefit of the lathe cut is that you can make a very small amount of them. You can make one (like the previously mentioned owner of the limited to one 'Oktave Dokkter' record) or any number above one. They are beautiful items. They are entirely DIY and totally made from love. The music is made from love, the person making the lathe cuts does it because they love it, and then you make a sleeve and you give them or sell them to people who will love them. In the past I've made a couple for people, I briefly ran a lathe cut label and released a couple of 10"s. I'm a massive fan of the lathe cut record.

But this release ended up being a normal record. A twelve-inch record, and 100 were made. It would have cost too much to make 100 lathe cuts, there is not a great economy of scale with the lathe cut. The normal financial rules do not apply.

'Witchfinder' was recorded before Rhys moved to Japan, he recorded it and mixed it. Then he moved. It was released while he was gone and they all sold out. I had to buy him a copy from eBay due to us blundering and not saving him a copy. We recorded it in Dropout. Our instruction to each other was: 'Let's do a fairly fast jam in C, have some ups and downs'. From the years of 2007-2013 that was how a lot of songs were recorded. Many didn't make it out to the real world. When they worked though, when we were all on point, we allowed them to venture out onto albums, compilation tracks and in this case a twelve-inch.

I had some questions for Pete Davis of OneC:

You ran a record label, why?

"It was something I wanted to do for a long time, I'd been in bands and we'd self-released stuff. I'd toyed with the idea of doing a label but ultimately never got around to it until an opportunity presented itself that allowed us to release a record. (A commission from Plymouth Arts Centre that was used to put together a compilation album of Plymouth-based bands doing sea shanties!)"

If you could do anything differently what would that be?

"Probably have been more careful about how many records to

get pressed up, that first record we had 500 pressed up. That's a lot of records to try and sell! And, out of all our back catalogue, it's one that I don't have a copy of! (scratching head). I should have trusted my instinct a little more on some of the releases, but sometimes you just get excited by the possibilities!"

We're really grateful you released the Witchfinder twelve-inch, do you have any hidden under your bed?

"Unfortunately not, I have one copy. The 'Witchfinder General' twelve-inch was one of those great ones that sold out in a couple of weeks. That was the way I liked to do things as it was a quick turn over and allowed for the next release to come out quickly".

What are you up too now?

"I'm in a band called Gad Whip. I didn't really have time to be in a band and do the label. And although the label was a great and fulfilling thing to do, it did cause some sleepless nights and a bit of stress."

Three records you'd save from a fire?

"No Means No, *Wrong*. Minutemen, *Double Nickels on the Dice*. Butthole Surfers, *Locust Abortion Technician*."

This answer took Pete half a second to come up with, the reply was instant, no delay at all.

The record was released in October of 2012. We had them for our appearance at Supersonic Festival in Birmingham. I was the only sober member of our party at this festival as I was driving and to my ears we played terribly. Such a shame. We sold all the copies of the twelve-inch though and that was it, they were gone. It was one of those shows where the sound was bouncing all over and the booze was beginning to ruin everything. You can't play subtly or with taste when you're drunk. It was OK when we were a more out there band but we were attempting to be more than that. I was frustrated.

By the middle of the next year, at 2013's Supernormal, I drank my last beer. Two things pushed me over the edge. One was seeing a group of people I knew being in such a mess. I felt like I was watching it from the outside. It had a huge effect on me, it was out of control and depressing. It's not the drinking, it's the not knowing when to stop. It's not the falling, it's the landing. The other was on the journey home, Elisa and I had gone together. She seemed so sad, there was one look that did it. I doubt I'll ever forget the look, it said all that was needed. So, August 9th, 2013 was the last time I drank any alcohol. My aim was to focus on family, work, and music and those three things alone, and do them to my very best ability. I was thirty-nine years old and that's old enough for anyone to know better.

Jon stopped six months before me, over the new year of 2012-2013. I guess we were both reaching that point. We both had to regain focus.

When we started the band, I was sober. In 2002 Elisa was pregnant with Freddie, our second and last (due to 2014's Valentine's present) son. He was born in April 2003. Stan had arrived in 2000, he's now better on the guitar than me and as tall as me. Freddie is getting to be the same height. We have photos of him as a two-year-old, with bands staying over and him looking baffled. When we were waiting for Freddie I stopped drinking to be part of the no-drinking-while-pregnant team. The band formed out of the energy one gets when one is sober. In 2013 when I stopped again, Tim, Roo and I started another band. Roo wanted to learn the drums so the three of us formed Henry Blacker. We've now released three albums and played almost 100 shows. It's easy to do as we all live in Somerset.

That's the choice for me, booze or bands. It's bands every day now. I still go into pubs when at work, delivering bills. The smell and feel is as enticing as it ever was. In the winter when the fire is going and there's an old boy sitting quietly with a pint I think to myself, is that me in thirty years' time? We recently walked past a bursting-to-the-seams boozer in Bristol, the smell that poured out attacked me and almost sent me back to the old days. My head spun 360, we headed for the ice cream parlour instead. I wasn't a whisky for breakfast person, but I did think about it a lot and it did influence a lot of decisions. In fact, I can't stop writing about it now. God damn. Booze is a drug, it's great. It destroys. It relaxes. It stresses. It costs.

'Witchfinder General Hospital' didn't remain out of print. The song ended up on the double vinyl compilation that MIE Records released in 2016, a best of the first ten years. Which itself was a reissue of a cassette that S.O.U.L (Sides Of Unequal Length)* pressed fifty copies for our tenth anniversary show in 2013. Of course, for those who collect records this wasn't 100 per cent satisfactory as the 'Witchfinder' twelve-inch, limited to 100, is still needed to complete the collection. We are sorry, keep checking Discogs or eBay. It'll turn up. I'm sure a few people

---

* The cassette label run by Philm Riot and Stuart Thompson who ran Victory Garden Records who released 'Ghost Ship' on the split seven-inch with the Phil Collins Three.

who bought it hate it. The compilation is called *Dedicated to Uri Klangers*. It wasn't until early 2018, five years after the initial cassette release, did anyone ask why it was called that. Uri was rhyming slang for Stella and Klangers related to the fact that most of our songs, before having proper titles, had temporary names like C Clanger or D Clanger. I think people thought Uri Klanger was a Communist hero or an extreme freedom fighter that they should have heard of. So they kept quiet. If you want a quick way into the first 10 years of this band then *Uri Klangers* is the portal. A lot of photos and words, two records, and tunes from all the releases, 2004-2013.

The Hey Colossus guide to touring

18

1

The night before you head off on your inevitable world domination-achieving four-date tour go to the supermarket and spend £30 on snacks and drinks for the whole band. Not just for yourself, who are you? Donald Trump? Buy bottled water, various fruit, nutty health bars, crisps and Maltesers for Rhys. By doing this you will save triple as to what you'll spend on the road. You won't need to stop for water the night after a heavy one. You may be able to make it to the next show without stopping for a service station lunch. We've never seen any other band do this and it's utterly baffling. You lot must have money to burn.

2

Aim for the earlier ferry. Ninety per cent of the time they let you on the earlier one, you don't get charged. If you miss your actual ferry you will be charged. Beat the system, stick it to the man, get the earlier ferry.

3

Your sat-nav says, 'Three hours to Paris', you tell the band 'It's five hours to Paris'. This way you get to the venue only one hour late.

4

If you're a miserable bastard when you don't get enough sleep; if you're a miserable bastard when the weed runs out and there's no more on the horizon; if you're a miserable bastard if a gig goes wrong, if no one turns up, if your gear breaks; if you're a miserable bastard in a van on a long journey; if you're a miserable and rude bastard to people you don't know; if you're a miserable bastard when you have no money; if you're a miserable bastard and you know it, then don't bother touring. Stay at home. You don't have to do it. You can not do it.

From 2014 onwards, we became determined to sort ourselves out. We began writing songs, actual real songs. Songs with different bits in, songs that had a planned flow. Rhys had moved back from Japan and climbed back onto the drum stool. Jon brought a lot of ideas in, I wrote one with my teeth. The song 'Wired Brainless' was a toothy tune, just two notes but it was the rhythm that hooked me in. For around a week I walked my round at work and this rhythm was cracking through my brain like a factory's worth of steel pressing machinery on full power. The two notes are open A (the second fattest string) and the 10th fret. They were played like this:

A-A-A-10-10-10-A-A-10-10-A-10. Looped forever.

You play them flat with a slight emphasis on the first note of each change. It was a numbers thing, I liked the numerical pattern of 3/3/2/2/1/1 so that's how it came about. My teeth clattered with it. It was a total of twelve beats. If you loop something round that has a division of four, three times, or something that has a division of three, four times, you can play it forever and no one gets bored. You're always finding new beginnings and endings; the guitars can alter and re-emphasise things.

Upon taking it to the band we played it like this for a while and it felt too much, so it ended up being just the first note of each change. Like this (imagine ghost notes happening where the dashes are):

A -- 10 - - A - 10 - A 10

Jon starts the song with the original full riff. Bob plays an AC/DC-esque couple of chords and Rhys plays a minimal beat on the toms. After a minute or so the bass comes in playing the line with just the first notes. Tim plays an echoey shuffling guitar part and Rhys adds snare and high hat. I love Jon's guitar lines and high clanging chords and I'm a massive fan of Paul's vocals.

The song is 100 times better than what I had in my head. The riff may have been the acorn, but the song would never have got to where it was without all the parts in play. If you ever play in a band or if you're thinking of doing so, always listen to everyone else. Always be open to change. Don't be utterly blinkered into thinking your way is the best. The same happened with 'Oktave Dokkter', the bass line was too much and needed to be stripped back. You will thank your bandmates for telling you you've gone way too overmuch. In the same way you thank your friends when they pull you back from a fight or the 10th pint. You may not thank them at the time, but the next day you're over the moon they stepped in and looked out for you.

As this band has moved the tactics have changed. Jon was searching for a way he could play within the set-up; in his early days we were route one, we made a lot of noise. Around the same time as our tactic change, I had a week with the New York composer Rhys Chatham in Liverpool. He was producing a piece of his called 'A Crimson Grail'. 100 six-string guitars, eight bass guitars and one drummer. We were divided into four groups of twenty-seven: two basses and twenty-five guitars. The drummer stayed by Chatham. Each group had its own conductor. We were set up around the Liverpool Anglican Cathedral, all playing through our own amps. Chatham conducted the conductors. He also had a soundperson who went around the room altering everyone's settings. We all ended up playing on virtually zero volume. I learned about tone, and about the power of a lot of people playing not very loud. The sound was still vast. The music was spread over so many octaves that it became a Hawaiian-sized wave of splendid noise. The cathedral acoustics created a swell. The sound climbed up the wall and dropped on the audience. A few thousand people showed up. The cathedral was such an awesome setting for this vast project.

Jon wanted to make his mark on our music, so we spread our tones out. The four guitars spread over the octaves, from left to right we went from high (Jon) to higher middle (Tim) to low (Bob) to lowest (me). We didn't need to play so loud anymore. Jon was now perfectly placed in a sound that suited his playing. The Rhys Chatham performance had opened my eyes. Both things happened at the same time. We found a format that worked for us, that worked for four guitars. The bass and drums stayed simple and tight, Bob stuck with me on our side of the stage, the high guitars stayed together on their side. They were playing trickier parts and could bounce off each other.

From this point, *In Black and Gold* onwards, we could create space and dynamics very simply: just drop out. If the high notes dropped out it went caveman with me and Bob. If the low notes dropped out it went tricky sounding and the rhythm changed.

Most people who play music like to play different sorts of music and vary it over numerous projects. Playing in Henry Blacker for instance, we're a three-piece noisy rock band very much in the late eighties-early nineties mould of Jesus Lizard and Kyuss. The three of us play it because we grew up with that music, we saw all those bands during our late teens and early twenties. That era of your life sticks with you. We do it because it's fun to play with friends. It's easy to travel as a three piece. It's fun writing as a band. I also like messing around with a four-track or a free program on the computer that I can plug a mic or guitar into. I do something with a fellow Somerset character called Kek. We call it Unruly Milk. We send files to each other and edit them and overdub things. Again, it's a fun thing to do. Neither of these, or Hey Colossus, are ever destined for super stardom. I firmly believe that once you get that idea, that playing music isn't about being mega famous, then you can enjoy music for the rest of your life. If you're somehow stuck with the mindset that reaching the top is the most important thing, you will give up very quickly. Your guitar will sit behind your bedroom door, then in the hallway, then into the loft or sold. Your dream forever unfulfilled.

The reason a song like 'Wired Brainless' is so perfect for me, and I'm not saying it's a perfect song for everyone, but for me it works is for this reason: I'm obsessed with music that can loop round and round. I like riffy bands and electronic music and all sorts but, ultimately, I like a loop that can hypnotize. Sitting on the sofa with a £25 acoustic guitar and playing round a guitar line that feels like it can play forever is one of the most relaxing things. There's a band from near Washington DC called Lungfish, they have this down to the finest art. Go look for their music. The simple sounding guitar lines will roll and roll, the rest of the band will join in and drop out. The vocals chant and sing. No band has been or will ever be as good at doing it as them. It doesn't stop me trying, sitting on the sofa looping lines around.

Stan, our oldest son, has Asperger's. He likes certain things in certain ways. One of the things he can do is zone out when under pressure. When going through a particularly stressful time he can switch off. When we moved to Somerset and he had to start a brand-new school Elisa had to go 'Hollywood' and wear shades. The tears were flowing. Stan though, he went into himself and walked into school. He had retreated to a distant place. We claim he's the most stoic person but it'll be the Asperger's and the fact he can use it to his advantage on occasion. He took his English GCSE exam a year early without realising. He can sometimes miss important information like 'You are now taking a GCSE exam'. I find it's possible to retreat to that place when playing a guitar line around and around, over and over, all else fades away and you get locked in. I guess all guitarists are the same (I am not a guitarist, not officially anyway. I hack at a bass but I'm woeful at six strings, but it doesn't stop me playing at home). Every now and then one of these little lines will make it into a song. 'Wired Brainless' was one of these. Two notes, looped. Chopped and edited. A total band song.

Rocket Recordings released this record. Chris Reeder and Johnny O'Carroll run the label. They are graphic designers and all the sleeves of the records they release have their touch. They look good on the shelves of shops, they've combined their two loves. The biggest band on their label is the band Goat, from Sweden. There are many bands called Goat. This one is the one that wear masks and full outfits and play a funky African inspired psych rock. I recently bought a record by a band called Goat, it was the Goat from Japan who play with an ultra-minimal style to achieve ultra-maximum results. There was a UK band called Goat who plied their trade around the time of Nirvana. They were of course grungy, somewhere I have a twelve-inch by them. I also like the band Goats. They were a hip-hop act from the second or third golden age of hip hop, depending on who you talk too. Seems naming your band Goat is a marker for success. We should change our name.

Rhys and Jon had released an album with Rocket before. Their band Notorious Hi Fi Killers' debut came out on the label. Tim F also had released something with Rocket when he was part of the band Spleen with Rob Ellis and a few others. Musicians and labels do this because they love it, it's the common theme. The netherworld. The upside down as Stranger Things would have you believe is a bad place, but this world of labels and bands that ninety-nine per cent of music lovers never see is coded. Once you crack the code you're in and you stay in. You get close to the music, you can watch the band and virtually be on the stage with them. The Garage in London had an upstairs. We saw a lot of bands there and I had a favourite spot. To the right of the stage there was a corridor that led to the toilets, and by standing in the corridor right by the stage you got the best sound. The onstage sound. There's many pictures of bands playing there with me lurking in the background, looking straight faced, absolutely focused on what's going on. My favourite is of the band Unwound, a three piece from America. I only saw them once, but I made sure I was right in amongst it. I'm tall, arguably too tall. I can't stand at the front for this reason so The Garage having this toilet corridor was perfect. In no one's way, outside the toilet where no one wanted to be, standing right next to the music.

For labels to last over twenty years, like Rocket or Riot Season. For musicians to keep going for the same amount of time. For all this to happen, for all the heartache, there must be a reason. Songs are only part of the puzzle. I think the same about art, a urinal in an art gallery is art. A urinal in a public convenience is a hole to pour piss into. Songs need to be surrounded by the right people. A label can help define a song. Once Rocket started releasing our music we were immediately playing psych festivals, having not done so for the previous twelve years. We never thought of ourselves as being a psych rock band. It hadn't even occurred to us. We thought we were punk rock. The label and the band create a unifying item. Chris Reeder from the label replied to a few questions:

I'm saying there's a code you need to crack to find the underworld of all the music you release, of the world we inhabit. Do you have the key? Do you have any tips to help people find it?

"I think it is all about trust. Bands come to us to release their music because they trust we will do our best (within our limited resources) with it. Whether that is the way it is presented regarding the artwork, or how we will promote it. We are not just a 'collectors label', releasing limited run records to just keep collectors happy. We always try and take a band and make them more popular than they were before they joined us. And I think bands appreciate that. I grew up watching *Top of the Pops, Chart Show* and *SNUB* and when an underground band I liked made it onto the TV, infiltrating the mainstream, it was a great moment and that has always stuck with me. I am a champion of the underground and DIY. Breaking these bands' music into the mainstream without sacrificing integrity or quality is something I drive for.

Also, it is the trust we have with our bands. When we start working with a band we have trust in them. We are with them for the journey of that release or for the several releases we may do with them."

Why did you start and why are you still going?

"I suppose because our passion for music and desire to be involved in the underground/DIY music scene was more than just being a listener/record buyer. What started it is probably the way most DIY labels start, a good friend of ours (Gareth Turner) was in a band called Lillydamwhite and someone had to release their music. if we didn't do it, who would? We had a real passion for the US DIY scene, labels like Sympathy of the Record Industry, Am Rep, Alternative Tentacles, Sub Pop singles club, In The Red etc and the way they did things was a huge inspiration to us when we started.

And why are we still going? Stubbornness. I don't know, I suppose it is down to the music we get given by bands.

I mean, the high quality of the music we get asked to release, has to be put out. So, in a way, each year blurs into the next as we are always six months to a year ahead in our planning. I suppose if the quality of music we were given stopped then I suppose we would to. We are only as good as our bands' music."

You both work and run the label, would you like to stop working to solely run the label or is working part of the reason the label is allowed to be fairly left field?

"Well, I was a full-time creative director for a design agency up until 2015, so I was juggling a very time consuming, full-time job and the label. But since then I have flipped that over, taking a massive pay cut. I now do the label full time and freelance design when I need some money. There is not enough money in Rocket to pay us both enough to go full time. But to be honest, I love design, so I am happy to freelance, it keeps the creative juices flowing.

And I don't know if this way we work has made us a more leftfield label. It is just who we are. We have many times turned down 'guaranteed sellers' to put out a more weird and wonderful and 'unlikely to sell many albums' release. The reasons are that we do not and ever want to put out 'beige' music. Yes, 'beige' sells but John and my tastes are far more colourful, and we basically release what we like. Not everyone likes all our releases, but that is fine. John and I have quite unique tastes and we are content our tastes are not for everyone. We don't want to be a noise label, we don't want to be a trad psych label, we don't want to be a metal label, we don't want to be an avant jazz label, we don't want to be a 'beige' indie label. We just wanna be a record label that puts out stuff we think is good."

Three records that you'd save?

"Adam and the Ants, *Kings of the Wild Frontier;* Mudhoney, *Superfuzz Bigmuff;* Can, *Soundtracks.* They each have their own story."

We were over the moon that Rocket wanted to do it, they worked with Paul on the sleeve and it looked incredible. It stands out. It has one of the most recognizable spines. Have a look at your record collection, all the spines are staring at you. There's always a few that stand out, they may be brightly coloured (Shonen Knife's self-titled record) or really wide (Can's *The Lost Tapes*) or have totally bold writing (Flower Travelling Band's *Sartori* LP). *In Black and Gold* is shiny. I have records that I've lost due to their bleak spine. It may only be three millimetres but don't forget your spine when nailing the art down. Rocket, the graphic designers, nailed this down. Rocket made us be a little more professional in our ways. They made us think about things we'd never thought of before like having good band photos and planning releases in advance, six months or so. Our band photos are still terrible, maybe we need to start wearing masks. We're not very good in front of a camera, we become awkward and nervous. Playing music in front of people is different to being in front of the camera. It's the reason we've never made a truly successful music video, none of us want to gurn for the camera. We can't do it. In fact, I don't trust people that can do it, or who want to do it. What the hell are you doing, what are you hiding, what are you running from? Your confidence and self-belief is freaking me out.

'Wired Brainless' was in the set for a couple of years, currently it isn't. I'm hoping to bring it back. It's a tricky song to play due to the bass line remaining the same and the drums and Jon's guitar doing a lot of the pick ups and drops. The vocals come in at specific places that require all the players to play the same thing as on the recording. Now the band's line up is slightly altered it's a big job to get it all back in place. A new guitarist listening to the recording can barely work out which guitar is doing what, it makes it hard to lock in. We have new songs that are the priority. Killing your loved ones is not easy, but in line with the marching on of time one must move on.

Through all the songs in this book and all the songs we've recorded we can't claim there haven't been influences. Some of the tunes have come fully formed, but even those get touched by the plectrums and drumsticks of the rest of the band. A song like 'Wired Brainless' is arguably the best example of all the band members playing to their strengths.

From the beginning we were keen on being a heavy band with repetition. This lasted for four years. We switched, in the year of 2007, to wanting to be both of those things but more frazzled. Then, after the *Cuckoo* LP, the decision was made to be more precise with our attack. Focus on the strengths, cut the chaff. It's been interesting to me as from the beginning we were being compared to bands I'd never listened too, and in some examples still haven't. Neurosis and Swans being the main two. When I'd tried to listen to them they seemed so serious. I can appreciate them now, they seem very professional. They seem to have no humour about them whatsoever, but I can appreciate them. They have some decent riffs and play with utter conviction. I can appreciate all that. I don't need a triple LP by either of them, but I can appreciate them. They are both bands on an entirely different level to us, so I know I'll never meet them, it's fine. Stan likes

Neurosis. Because he likes them I'll end up liking them. I'll end up regretting not buying their records and not seeing them, and then, ultimately, I'll regret not being more serious about what we do.

I have always liked heavy music, but it must have some element of fallibility too it. The bands covered in heavy music magazines, all posing with grim faces and black T-Shirts, haven't done it for me since I was fifteen. I went to Castle Donnington for the Monsters Of Rock festival when I was fourteen, even then I probably looked a little aghast at the whole situation. My dad took me and a friend, Phil Plested (I see Phil very occasionally. He's stunned we still do band stuff. That's the thing when you meet old school friends and you've not grown out of the thing you were banging on about when you were twelve). For ten hours bottles of piss flew over our heads while men with big hair in Saxon T-Shirts headbanged to Megadeth, who were rubbish. Then they headbanged to Kiss, who were rubbish. David Lee Roth was fun, but the piss bottles somewhat took away the feeling that we could totally relax into his set. Iron Maiden were Iron Maiden. I have a soft spot for Iron Maiden, they're hilarious and I think they know it, they have some massive tunes though. 'Run to the Hills' is undeniable. Someone died while Guns N Roses played. They were on first. When the line-up was booked they weren't that big of a band. By the time it came around 'Sweet Child O'Mine' had become a big song and they were the most hyped rock band on the planet. There was a crush when they played and it all went wrong.

I need some human element. I'm not into rock stars. The problem with heavy metal is the need for the band people to look like, and pose like, and play like, rock stars. If I were to list my favourite big heavy bands it'd be along these lines (please bear in mind this list is a through the ages list. Some from back when I was a lot younger, who have stood with me through the years): Black Sabbath, Melvins, Faith No More, AC/DC, Anthrax, Primus, Voivod, Soundgarden (specifically Ultramega OK and Louder Than Love – these two records are goofy/heavy/non-rock star rock) and Janes Addiction. These bands, to me, despite being massive in some examples, all come across as being non-rock star. The idea of big rock bands being non-rock star may seem contradictory, but the cliché of the rock star is so worn out. Chris Holmes pouring vodka into himself while in his swimming pool, overlooked by his aghast mother, is entirely of a different era. Do take the time to watch *Decline Of The Western Civilization Part II** if you want an idea of where it all went wrong in the late 1980s.

By the time I was sixteen I'd moved away from being a heavy metal purist.

I'm grateful to have grown up when I did. I didn't get email until I was twenty-five. The internet didn't impinge on my life properly until my late twenties. We had to scour the music press for information. We had pen friends gained from the back of

---

* Here's the debunking moment hinted at pages and pages ago: Stan has watched this film. He likes to look things up, he likes to learn. He looked up this film. The Chris Holmes scene is, apparently, a fake. His bottle is full of water not vodka. Also, the scene where Ozzy supposedly pours orange juice all over his kitchen table was filmed after, using someone else's hand, and edited in. Even these film-maker tricks, if true, help sum up the glitz and glamour and totally vacuous nature of late 1980s LA metal. Nirvana couldn't come soon enough.

music magazines who we'd trade tapes with, both cassette and video. If I bought a record off the back of a review. If I spent all my paper round money on it and had travelled to Shades Records (a heavy metal record shop of some repute, St. Annes Court, Soho. It's not there anymore. I think it's now a hairdressers) and back on a Saturday afternoon to get it. If I then got home with it, put it on the turntable and it was rubbish I would make damn sure I kept listening too it until I liked it.

A prime example of this is the French/Canadian band Voivod's *Dimension Hätross* album. It came out in 1988. I would have bought it around then, aged fourteen or fifteen. Kerrang would have reviewed it and claimed it to be the best record ever, or some other hyperbole. So that was me, spending my £10 paper round money to get into central London. Walk to Shades. Buy the record. Walk back to the station. Get the train home and put the record on the turntable. It took me weeks to get into *Dimension Hätross*. The vocals were not what I was used too. The playing was not what I was used too. The song structures and overall sound were so far away from Iron Maiden or Anthrax I was left baffled. But I persisted. I question whether that persistence exists now. There's no need. You can listen to an album before buying it. You can dismiss it before it seeps into your soul, it won't get a chance. I'm suspicious a lot of records are not getting loved with the same depth.

Voivod, and this album, have been a consistent influence on me over the last thirty years. They made me listen to music with an open mind, they made me not judge on first listen. The exact same thing happened with the Janes Addiction album, *Nothings Shocking*. An excellent review in a music paper, me spending my money, me then spending months trying to get into it. The space and oddness of Nothings Shocking was eye opening. The sleeve even had to be covered up by a rubber outer sleeve due to its supposed offensive nature (it's not offensive in the slightest, certainly not when compared with eighty per cent of all other rock and metal album sleeves of the time). I can listen to either of these records now and I get a flashback to those days. I remember the effort it took. I appreciate the fact that young me put the time in.

We may sound nothing like either of these bands, but the influence is taken from the bravery to release the records they wanted to release. To have the faith to go with their guts in a heavy metal field littered with cliché and rules.

My love of repetition in music doesn't come from a source that has ever been mentioned in reviews. It's always assumed if you play guitar music and you play the same thing again and again you're going to be a big Krautrock fan. I do like those bands. They're fine. They pushed the sound of music. You can hear them in most current big bands from Coldplay to Primal Scream. All the big bands claim a love of these German innovators. I have a fair amount of their records, I particularly like the Can's *Lost Tapes* box set. But my big thing is rap music. I'm more obsessed with that than any legendary German band.

The production in rap music is inspiring. There's a lack of ego to it. The music makers often go unheralded with the vocalist taking all the plaudits. Which is probably how both parties like it. To make the music and the beat for rap music you need to account for the vocal. You need to keep it unobtrusive but bring the funk. You need to make it so it stands on its own, it needs to be inspired. You need a vast music knowledge. You need to dig through crates of records from around the world to find the best beats. These producers are similar to techno producers in that anonymity is an option most choose. I can listen to instrumental hip hop tracks and take so much from them.

My favourite producer, who has consistently provided me with joy and inspiration, is Erick Sermon. He is one half of the group EPMD (Erick and Parrish Making Dollars, Parrish Smith being the other half). The group's first five records are all landmarks in production. Their vocal style was distinctive. They were self-proclaimed hardcore rap, any success they got was gained through the underground and building it up. When they split most assumed Parrish Smith would go on to be the bigger of the two, his vocal style was more traditional. But it was Erick Sermon's production that stood proud. There's a tune from Sermon's fifth solo record called 'Relentless'. This one tune has been a constant in my life. Any doubts I have I return to it and listen to the way the one bass line loops letting other things alter around it. Letting it sit in the pocket. Letting it do its thing. There's a couple of guitar samples that bounce off each other. I can hear HC doing this song. Maybe not the vocal. I'll speak to Paul and get back to you. Sermon's vocal delivery is as the song title implies, relentless, he's ranting against the music industry. About how he's been ignored, basically giving a big fuck you to all the major players. Hip hop has a habit of forgetting the legends, always looking to the new, forgetting the old. This song is about that. The bass line rolls, the tune is pure anger and solid funk. There's no chorus. The hook is in the bass. I can't talk about EPMD as there aren't enough words for me to say how important they are to me, but this tune sums Erick Sermon and EPMD up.

Other examples of the background producer barely getting the credit, but being at least fifty per cent of the song, include Clams Casino. Have a listen to his instrumental work, created in his loft in New Jersey, then used by A$ap Rocky to make him who he is. Or check out London's Ruff Sqwad with their instrumental tune 'Functions On The Low', then listen in as Stormzy freestyles over it a decade on with his tune 'Shut Up'. Or, have a listen to Action Bronson and Riff Raff's track 'Bird on a Wire', look at them strolling the streets in their expensive gear and smoking and looking tough. But take it as a given that the music was knocked together by an indoor nerd, in this case Harry Fraud.

It's the lack of ego. The band should be ego-less. The band should be concentrating on nailing the track. Let everything else take care of itself. Stop the posing. It's the music that lasts.

Notice how I've not mentioned J Dilla here. He's on another level to everyone. If you don't know J Dilla, start digging. Get his record *Donuts* and work from there. An album created from a hospital bed and made to stand the test of time. He was in a race with himself, three steps ahead until the day he died.

Oh, you wanted to know what my top five rappers/rap groups are currently, active, in 2019?

1. Aesop Rock
2. Danny Brown
3. Earl Sweatshirt
4. Wiki
5. Run The Jewels

The repetition in tunes like Erick Sermon's 'Relentless' are why I'm happy to sit on one line through a song like 'Wired Brainless'. Rhys is a huge Michael Jackson and funk fan, he also produces acid techno under the Acidliner name so is locked in with me on the single bass line idea. He brings it up and down. On 'Wired Brainless' Bob is playing a couple of AC/DC-style chords that, along with bands like Snuff or Guided By Voices, are his bag. The three of us leave Tim and Jon to go off, and Paul has the space for his vocal. I like that no one picks up on where we're coming from as it's the end result that matters.

Earlier on I mentioned a couple of heavy albums (Godflesh and Anthrax) I wrote about for the Louder Sound website, regarding influential records. The rest are here. I'm including the EPMD one, even though it may cover similar ground to a few paragraphs back. No group deserves more coverage.

Dead C - Secret Earth

Nothing sounds like this band, and that is inspiration enough. Doing your own thing, finding a different route. A three-some from New Zealand. Together for thirty-plus years now, with numerous releases of which I am missing a fair few. This one is probably my favourite. They have the sound of three people who have only ever played music with each other, have grown with each other and exist outside of all other rock music.

There's a truly splendid little film called *27 Minutes With Mr Noisy* about Bruce Russell, made by his daughter. He takes you on a little trip around their home town of Dunedin. Taking in the old venues and their old houses. It's sort of beautiful and well worth checking out. It has a slight 'at odds with the world feel' which I can't quite put my finger on. The Dead C's music makes me want to make music that is like no other. An ambition that is rather grand and pretty much unobtainable. Unless you're the Dead C.

Fugazi - Margin Walker

You can tell the age of your copy of this record by the amount the post-paid price is on the rear of the sleeve. There's no band that has meant more to me than this band. This is the first record I bought by them. It was picked up from Oven Ready Records, High Wycombe, on a family shopping trip on a Saturday afternoon around 1990. I was an avid heavy metal magazine reader. One of those must have reviewed them as I cannot think how else I would have checked them out. I remember digging into Kyuss at the same time purely because there was a photo of the band playing live. The guitarist was wearing Vans, which weren't quite so ubiquitous back then.

When this record starts, and the guitars do that harmonic slide scrape over the bass. That in itself was remoulding what you should do with guitars in a punk rock band. I cannot tell you how much those few seconds changed what I thought in regards the job specifications of the guitar. I'm not sure I can even argue that it's the best Fugazi record, although it could be to me. Listening now, and I heartily recommend everyone puts down what they're doing and does the same, you can hear the sound of positive action. The sound of a band tearing off on their own, stripping the whole thing down to the nuts and bolts. You don't need them, you can do it for you and do it for your crew. My copy of this record is $5 post paid, and I'd buy it again and again and again.

DJ Rashad - Double Cup
When you avidly consume music, I'm convinced it's because you're after that high you experienced aged eight. Back when you first heard Rod, Jane and Freddy or whatever children's programme you used to watch, while whoever was looking after you was sleeping or making lunch or whatever. Finding new sounds is key. You can't keep buying the same music style and expect to be stunned time and again. This record was one that

came out of nowhere for me. Sound-wise it was baffling. Having watched numerous YouTube documentaries about the Footwork/Juke scene out of Chicago, I'm sort of still none the wiser. But I will say it blows me away. The cut-up rhythms, the crazy energy, and the dancing. Which, for the record, I don't traditionally do. So, when I went to see Jlin play up in Bristol a year or so back, I was fairly stunned to find myself shuffling back and forth. This record is, in my very limited knowledge of the scene, a total banger and well worth the entrance fee. Jlin's *Dark Energy* record and DJ Roc's *The Crack Capone* are also worth picking up. It's all about finding new highs, not getting trapped in the same scene. You gotta keep moving.

The Fall - Your Future Our Clutter

A fairly recent (2010) Fall record. I reckon it makes it into their top five records, which I realise is a bold statement. Let me clarify, I love The Fall. I got into them around the release of *Code: Selfish,* then had to work backwards while also following their onward path. It's not easy doing this. They release a lot. It's for this reason (along with their stubborn excellence) that they're included in this list. Bands with vast discographies who crash on through are like cobwebs holding the music industry up. You need them. The Fall are important because Mark E Smith* is so gruesomely snarky. He's so riddled with history and virtually always musically correct when guiding his ship. This record bubbles with bluster. Personally, for the last 15 years or so, it's the bass on The Fall's records that has me tuned in. It's distorted and belligerent, happy to sit on one or two notes. On this record it thunders like no other.

* This was written weeks before Mark died, RIP M.E.S

Check the tune 'Bury Pt.s 1 and 3', when it drops in. Oh man. The whole band is on form, and for that to be the case 34 years in, to create a maelstrom like this, is medal-worthy. All should aim to build up a discography like it. Raise a glass to Lancashire's finest.

Braid - The Age Of Octeen
I got this record around 1998, it had already been out for a couple of years. There wasn't such a rush to keep up with stuff back then. The internet wasn't judging you for not owning something. No daily emails from record shops telling you a new 'best release this month' is out. Or that it's 'sold out at source'. Whatever. I was into bands like Rites Of Spring and the aforementioned Fugazi. I was working at Southern Records for free because I loved music and had no problem being ripped off.

Southern distributed Polyvinyl Records. The album after *Age of Octeen, Frame and Canvas,* came out via them while I worked there. Which is how I learned about the band. I was late to the party. Braid were touring Europe to promote their new record. The people who worked at Southern put a gig on in Gypsy Hill, South London (famous pretty much only for the Hard Skin lyric "Betting on the dogs down Gypsy Hill, William Hill is fucking skill"). They played with The Get Up Kids, The Tone and Mouthwash. I picked this record up, the band's second, at that show. It's on Mud Records. It has that old-school mid-80s emo sound. Like what Moss Icon or the UK's Bob Tilton were peddling. Both of whom could have made this list, actually.

This record was perfectly-timed for when we started our own label (Jonson Family) and released our band's first seven-inch (Stanton, *Four Walls*). We made very vague attempts to be something like this and Sebadoh. The doing-it-yourself incentive came from going to that gig and owning records from that world. The show itself is probably one of the greatest I've seen.

EPMD - *BusinessNever Personal*

I've found your favourite record by a band or artist is often the first record you buy by them. Irrespective of the common consensus, you stand by the first record you buy. Like, for instance, *Goo* is my favourite Sonic Youth record. I know ninety per cent of people would say *Daydream Nation* or *Sister.* This is EPMD's fourth album, it's the first I bought by them. I got into it while retaking my GCSEs at college. A friend at the time, Adrian, was a rap guru. He had hundreds of records (hundreds was lots when you were 17). Every single one of them was a rap record. The one he played the most, and had two copies of, was this album. He had one for scratching with, he would show me with pride the total state of his scratched up copy, and one for playing. He would talk me through it, explain how it was made and I ate up his knowledge.

Erick Sermon's production on this record, and all the other EPMD records and his solo stuff, is so different to most others. He runs the funk just behind the beat, which suits my slow mind down to the ground. If you want an example check the tune 'Chill' from this record. It sounds like it's slipping. The track is so laid back, but him and Parrish Smith destroy it on the mic. The slight builds on the chorus and the drop back on the verses. Total head-nodding shit.

Cypress Hill - *Cypress Hill*

I'm not an old-school 'rap is the best', golden age of hip hop sort of person. Recent excellence has come from Kendrick Lamar, Earl Sweatshirt, Run The Jewels, the last Tribe Called Quest record, and many others. But in terms of influence, the debut Cypress LP is untouchable. I read about them, probably at Adrian's house. He had all the HHC mags. Then bought it in Track Records, Chesham (where I worked in the Perfect Pizza – dream job). It was 1991 or maybe 1992, and it was such a bolt of lightning. DJ Muggs' production was so radical. The hefty funk with the high wails and squeaks and of course B-Real and Sen Dog were the perfect mix of high pitch whine versus low-rider grind.

I got to see them twice around then. They played a small stage at the Phoenix Festival (Normski introduced them). It was in a tent, they were first on. The tent was rammed and it kicked off like a punk rock gig. Hugely eye opening to see the way they got the tent bumping not using guitars, very refreshing. Then around the same time they played with House Of Pain and Funkdoobiest in Brixton and it was the same deal, carnage. Muggs' productions soon got played out, but for a brief couple of years it was the sound. Now when I go on about this record people say their second album is the one, but for me the debut is the moment where they had all the energy and were creating something new.

Lungfish - Talking Songs For Walking
Standing watching Lungfish at the ATP Festival 10 or so years back with Elisa. We had been listening to the band for 10 years beforehand and never thought we'd see them. We'd spent so many nights listening to them we almost named our first son Samuel because of the song Samuel. As we were standing there, I swear to God it was dust in my eye. You want a band? This is a band. I know they would argue they'd done better records than this one. They did get slightly more minimal, but that rhythm remained, the Lungfish rhythm. This is the record that we played

and played and played. You can take so much from them. The precision of the playing, the economy of the playing, the repetition that never bores but instead brings you up, and the Higgs.

Daniel Higgs. Now there's a frontman. The day of the ATP show he was walking along the beach with his big coat on and his big beard on and his big hand tattoos on. Then he was standing there playing and all of it was a massive deal to us because we'd listened to this record so many times. It was on my favourite label. They were the longest-running band on the label. I'm sure as time goes on every single day a few more people will fall for them, and then eventually they will be our Wyld Stallion and unite this planet and all other planets.

And finally. During my brief time at college, once I'd retaken my GCSEs, I fell into doing a Btec in media production. The ultimate course for those who had no idea what they were going to do with their life but didn't want to go to work yet. For one term at college one of the lessons was on the music industry. The chap who taught it, wearing an ill-fitting suit, worn out T-shirt and Converse All Star trainers, was Steve Lake. He got us to design a record sleeve and go through how we would market the band. I designed a sleeve for a made up ska band called Ska'd For Life. There is almost certainly a ska band called Ska'd For Life. Modern day ska bands love a crumbling pun. My marketing plan was weak, my sleeve design was cliché. Steve Lake was, and still is, the bass player and songwriter in the post punk/anarcho group Zounds. Zounds have the right feel. They're of that time, production wise, but stand up to all what today can throw at them. It wasn't the course or my work that sparked my interest. It was the fact you can be in a band that moves people and it can be part of your life.

Not all of your life. You can be a teacher or a fireman or a nurse as well as doing music. Music is almost everything to me but it's most definitely not actually everything.

And finally, finally, finally, I must mention the enormous and wide-ranging world of punk and DIY rock. I feel like it's such a big topic that maybe I'll ask if I can write an entire book on the subject. (Note to self: Do this). We all take deep inspiration from the bands we play with and tour with. Those that don't worry about chasing success. Those that see playing music as the all-encompassing social experience that it is. From the US underground of the 1980s through to today's myriad of scenes throughout Europe and beyond. The following song, 'Hey, Dead Eyes, Up!' touches on everything I've written about in this section. It has the same bass line that plays throughout. It has the drums that pick up. The guitars sound like they're lifted from any classic post punk record. The vocals are hugely satisfying. We can all mouth along, thinking we know the words like one of the people in Black Flag that isn't Morris or Reyes or Cadena or Rollins. I'd dedicate it to all the bands who are running in the same race as us, but it would be cheesy as hell to do so.

HEY, DEAD EYES, UP!
from In Black And Gold
2015

Dear bands, you have a forty-minute set, you have a thirty-minute set. You have been given an amount of time to play your songs. You start at 10pm, you finish at 10.30pm. You start at 8pm, you finish at 8.40pm. Other bands may be playing after you. The crowd have patiently watched your set. Although it isn't all about you, you do get an amount of time to impress people. Use the time wisely. Make all the noise you want in your allotted slot. Start on time, finish on time. Have respect for the audience, have respect for the promoter, have respect for the venue. Crush everyone with your wit, amaze all with your bombast. Stun the world with your riffs and syncopated 5/4 rhythms. Change the direction of humanity with your lyrical prowess. Inspire people to pick up a drum machine or guitar or microphone.

But, when your time is up, please stop. Have a song in your set that has an ending. Leaving your guitars feeding back as you sweatily climb off the stage to the adoring tens of people is tiresome for everyone. You are not being punk rock. You haven't destroyed the room. You haven't left a pile of rubble. You're more than likely stumbling off the stage to 27 people all waiting for the next band, all wishing they'd stayed at home.

'Hey, Dead Eyes, Up!' (written on set lists, and known only as, 'Dead Eyes') is our song where we all end at the same time. We stop on a dime. It's the end. No feedback, no nothing. We stop, we pack our gear up, we get out of the way for the next band. We've learned that people want you to stop. We're not unrealistic. Even if all the thirty people are baying for more they don't mean it, they're taking part in the standardized gig ritual. They would die a little inside if you came back on and played a song that wasn't good enough to make it into your actual set.

I would argue that most people only have around two or three bands they would watch more than forty minutes of. Mine, if you're interested, are Fugazi, AC/DC and Lungfish. I could probably handle forty-five minutes of Fleetwood Mac. Recently Freddie, Elisa and I went to see Run The Jewels and they were good for forty-eight minutes. You get given time to play, use it wisely. Don't overstay your welcome and for the love of all that's evil give it a break with the feedback* as you leave the stage. Aside from anything else you've got to come back on and switch it off. Making you look like an attention seeking, never heard of the MC5, fool.

Jon brought the ideas in for this tune, the man was on fire. It's not very long and is essentially one riff although I'm not sure

* In the very unlikely event you're unaware of this, feedback is when a guitar is left with its volume on full near the amp. It will create a wailing noise. It sounds like an old skool kettle whistle or any other sort of whistle that goes on and on and on. Someone like Hendrix used it in an artful masterful way. Your man in Jimmy Fucknut and the Lovepumps is, I would argue, not using it in an artful way. He believes he's just destroyed the room. He thinks he's created aural armageddon and you will never forget this moment. His guitar is prostrate on the stage. The sound of a 1970s kettle boiling. The 27 people in the room are chatting amongst themselves.

people realise this. We're reasonably firm believers in one main riff per song. Strip it back, emphasize different notes, switch the rhythm, keep the main riff trucking through. Rhys has a knack for dropping off and picking up, we all follow him. On this tune I get huge satisfaction from the open fat string, tuned to C (as previously mentioned). I use it when the main riff is at its heaviest, I don't use it when Paul is singing the verses. It's not that I get louder, but I do love the low note not being there all the time. The opening riff is very metal, especially once both Jon and Tim are playing together, the tune is gnarly.

The end part, where we all (apart from Bob, more on this in a second) simply play the root notes in a triumphant song ending fashion, came about by accident. Jon, Tim and I play the 'triumphant' notes. It sounds like it was planned but it wasn't. We all cringed a little thinking it sounded like Linkin Park. Bob didn't do the notes, he stuck with the riff. He missed the telepathic nod. We listened back and thought about it, it sounded funny and righteous, so it stayed. Now when we play it live Bob carries on playing the riff and the rest of us raise our axes to the ceiling and hail Satan, or whoever.

In 2015 we played our biggest ever show, July 25th to be precise. I dream we match it one day. I'm an eternal optimist but I struggle to believe we'll get close. Anthony who runs the Baba Yaga nights in London, we have played many, was involved in choosing some UK bands to play at the Milhões De Festa in Portugal. We got lucky. On the 24th we played in London with Gnod. The morning after we flew to Porto. We were picked up and driven an hour north to the little town of Barcelos which sits on the River Cavado. We were taken straight to a hotel. As we pulled in The

Bug was just leaving. We've spent many journeys listening to this man's music. He was wearing some Beats headphones is all I remember. An hour or so later another van came and picked us up, we were taken to the site. It was around 4pm, our friend's band Grumbling Fur were playing on the main stage. The place was vast, it took us ten minutes to walk from the entrance to near the stage. We were told, 'You're on at 2am'. Have you ever been a Brit abroad with ten hours to kill and unlimited free beer? This was the situation we found ourselves in. It was mine and Jon's job to keep the other four from straying too far from being sober-ish people. We walked them around the town, we pointed at things, we showed them the river, we encouraged them to watch other bands.

It was hot. It was very hot. It was Portugal hot. Portugal may be in the same time zone as the UK but we were learning it was in a totally different league temperature wise.

A reminder: We were on at 2am.

UK bands like to be in bed by midnight. We like to play at 10, pack up, drive home, and be in bed.

On before us was Michael Rother, one of the main characters from the German band Neu! We all love the German band Neu! As, it seemed, did all of Portugal. We stood by the side of the stage and glanced out into the crowd, it was rammed. All up the hill. When the light shone out 5000 faces beamed back. As enjoyable as his music was, and it really was very lovely, it was somewhat tinged by the knowledge that we were on next and our money was on the fact that no one here had heard of us. Rother finished his set to rapturous applause. Then we began setting up. There was a road crew scurrying around us, plugging things in and packing things away. We weren't used to having help. It was nice though.

We checked everything was working and looked out onto a vast empty field. The place had cleared out. 2am in Portugal must be bedtime.

As we began to make noise the field miraculously began filling up and by the end of the first song it was back to Rother levels. There were two stages at Milhoes, the band on the other stage had finished so the people came flooding back. I broke a string in the first song which was purely down to playing too hard through nerves. Luckily Anthroprophh were over and I borrowed Gareth's hot as hell Rickenbacker bass. The set went well. Have you ever played in an FA Cup Final? If so, you'll know what it's like when the manager says, 'Make sure you enjoy it' and, 'it'll all be over in a flash'. That's exactly what happened. The set was made up of songs from *In Black And Gold* and *Radio Static High* (which was yet to be released but seeing as no one here knew us from Adam we assumed, correctly, that it didn't matter. Just play the best tunes. Don't worry. *Make sure you enjoy it*). We ended the set with 'Dead Eyes' and the dust rising from all the dancing will stick in my mind forever. A mosh pit sandstorm rose up.

We were home before we knew it, back in Somerset, back in London. Then back at work on Monday. I try to not talk about band things at work. People take the piss. I would expect nothing less. The sorting office is a bloodbath. For years people japed about the lack of success and pointlessness of playing in a band. Then one Saturday morning Frank Skinner played a song of ours. The following Monday, as a couple had heard it while out delivering, the comments changed to be along 'Billy-big Bollocks' lines. Totally fair enough as I was now driving into work in a Hummer, burning money as fuel. I couldn't even begin to describe being flown to Portugal and playing a show like this, it'd come across as utter fantasy.

The breakfast is included in our hotel stay. To repeat: The. Breakfast. Is. Included. Is there anything better than a splendidly stocked buffet breakfast at a hotel?

We milk the fact we can stay in the hotel until noon, safe in the knowledge it's only two hours to the next city. Liege is a place we've played four or five times before, in a variety of venues. The first and second times were at La Zone, these were during the debauchery years. You sleep in the venue and the alcohol is endless. One of the nights was christened, by Jon, as the 'Night Of A Thousand Beers'. I have no idea whether we were any good at the shows, I doubt any of us have any idea whether we were any good at the shows. It feels such a long time ago, a different life. We've played twice in a venue called Le Garage which is an industrial unit converted into a venue. The sound bounces round but you only need 100 people to fill it to soak the sound up and the atmosphere is good. The other spot we played with Teeth of the Sea, CPCR, was an adult education centre/anarchist spot/all-round good place to help the community. Tonight, we play in a big professional hall that holds 550 people called Reflektor. It has a balcony and a backstage area bigger than any of the venues we've played before in this town. It looks and sounds like what your parents probably imagine a venue to be.

Backstage we discuss Chris Holmes, ex of the band W.A.S.P. We talk about his solo career. If you're unaware of Chris Holmes' solo career post W.A.S.P check it out. It contains many talking points, most of which we covered. Some careers of rock stars, post their big band, are very much worth paying attention too. Joe from Sumac struggles to find some Youtube footage for Rhys. Rhys is stunned. I have mentioned Chris Holmes a few times now. I must be obsessed.

The gig is decent, it's our fourth day in a row and we're a slick rock machine. Bob's guitar only cuts out once. Which as you can no doubt tell by the fact I'm making a note of it, is greatly noteworthy. Mr 'Inescapable' shows up in the crowd. He's a Nottingham-based Coventry City fan from Wales. His wife is from Stuttgart. He has convinced his family that they should go to Stuttgart for a holiday and he'll make his own way down. He'll come via the League two Play-Off final (Coventry City 3 Exeter 1) and via Liege to see us. He'll be in Stuttgart tomorrow as well. This time with his wife. It's going to be interesting to meet his wife. He got his name from shouting the word 'Inescapable' throughout shows. If you're from the Midlands, UK, you may be aware of his work. It started at an Echo and the Bunnymen concert. Singer Bunnyman got him kicked out for shouting it. So, now, it gets shouted all the time. I wonder if singer Bunnyman has any experience dealing with naughty children. Sometimes it's better to ignore a problem rather than draw attention to it. As Elisa says, you must pick your battles with children. Mr Inescapable is a diamond.

We are spread over the two promoters' houses. Three at Pierre's and four at Hadrien's. The four west country dwellers are at Hadriens. His house is spread over five floors. It's enormous and spectacular and we're all jealous. It cost him and his wife, Claire, 230,000 euros. To confirm, for those that spent time with the vidiprinter to get the football results when a miraculous 8-2-style result would come through, I just typed 'two hundred and thirty thousand euros'. It was a wreck and they're doing it up, they're halfway to being done. We're all toying with moving to Liege. Both Hadrien and Claire are teachers. Teachers who put on shows. Teachers who put on shows by bands containing postmen, departmental education charity workers, copywriters and warehouse workers. Teachers who put shows on in venues that hold 550 people. You can take what you want from these facts.

To repeat something from pages and pages ago: we love staying in hotels, but when you stay in someone's house you learn so much more. You take so much more away from your time. The memories are stronger.

HOP THE RAILINGS
from Radio Static High
2015

We thought it'd be hilarious to release two albums in a year. It almost killed us as a band. Rocket were into the idea but there was a deadline. A lot of tense emails were fired around for six months. Why we put ourselves through it I have no idea.

'Hop The Railings' was a Jon tune. He'd sent round a demo version of it. All I do is play two notes, everyone else does the good stuff. We got daytime radio play with this tune. It was all very exciting for almost eight days. Lauren Laverne played it two or three times, maybe four. She even replied to a Tweet. We were big-time for a week. The reality though was that we were all either just shy of forty or just over forty and it had taken twenty years to get a daytime play on any station anywhere. It was exciting, but it didn't last. We didn't record a radio session, no one asked. We still got no press and we still played the same shows. No festivals came knocking. I do wonder if we were the sort of people who mingled with people, if we hung out at the right places, if we had a manager who did this, whether any of it would have made a difference. In all honesty none of us really cared enough, we were all at work when radio plays happened.

When we moved to Somerset we stopped the record label we were running. It's hard to keep in touch when you wake up to the sound of sheep and cows. We were out of it, we stopped going to as many gigs. You can't run a good record label if you don't go out. I still go to shows in Bristol but I'm now the old weird guy at the back who sometimes gets there too early and looks awkward. I love live music. I enjoy going on my own if the music is a little bit off the wall. I went to see Wolf Eyes on my own. I enjoy not having to explain to someone that it sounds like it does because that's what they want it to sound like. I wouldn't want to be with someone else when one of Wolf Eyes, who are all my age or older, roll across the stage on a skateboard like a wizened Marty McFly. The age of the music fan is now wider than it used to be. The age of band people is also wider. We think about it a lot. We talk about it and laugh like hell at our age. It means nothing any more, to us. Lord only knows what young people think. We play shows and there can be older bands, but often we can play with a band of people who are all half our age. I dread to think what's going through their minds.

When daytime 6Music picked up on 'Hop The Railings' it was a strange time. We weren't writing music especially for daytime plays. This song is pretty easy on the ear though, and to this day is enjoyable to play live. It has a Talking Heads-New Order feel. It's sparse. We play it tight and with economy. This was a development, to use space as a weapon.

Because we've all spent years playing to no crowds we probably come across as a band enjoying it for ourselves. Bob and I still play angled towards the drums as if in a rehearsal or at an empty show. If people show up I'm very grateful and it makes me happy to see a few folk having fun, but I just love playing. I enjoy rehearsing the songs in a room when it's just the six of us. I take nothing for granted. Cities have a lot going on, us coming to town and playing is possibly the eighteenth best thing happening in town that night. We're up against a *Star Wars* trilogy at the Prince Charles cinema, a pub quiz three doors down, a free show at Rough Trade by the latest hot thing, curry night at Wetherspoons, a football match on TV, the unseasonably hot weather. If you choose to come and watch us, then you've had to cross a few excellent choices off the list of options for that night. We're grateful. A song like 'Hop' is good for this, it's as party as we go. It's a route one dancefloor banger. Larry Levan would have played it. If only. In our dreams. It's propelled along nicely by a straight motorik beat and a couple of notes on the bass. Bob plays just the one note but works his Wah Wah pedal up and down a bit. The two other guitars do a little more, creating the movement, and Paul sings.

I've taken both Stan and Freddie to gigs. It's a little sad that for the most part only big events operate a fourteen-plus door policy. The smaller venues are eighteen-plus and are strict about it. I took Stan to see Slayer and Anthrax. It's a parent's job to bring their child to at least one gig, however embarrassing it is for both parties. Slayer and Anthrax destroyed, to use the sort of terminology they probably use. Elisa and I have taken Freddie to see Kendrick Lamar and Run The Jewels. Introducing your offspring to live music is important and enjoyable. It's what you have left to bond over once your young children turn into slouching teenagers. All these big arena shows were big events in big rooms to big crowds, as you'd imagine. They start on time. They finish on time. They cost mortgage threatening amounts to get into. The T-Shirts are stunning in their price. How they have the nuts to charge what they charge is almost applaudable. The difference between the arena show and the 100-200 capacity show is so obvious it's barely worth mentioning. But to show the alternative I took Freddie to see Wiki, a New York rapper, recently signed to XL. He was playing at The Thekla in Bristol. Around 200 people were there, and we were within touching distance of the stage. Wiki ripped it the hell up. We could see the whites of his eyes. Similarly, Elisa brought Stan to see us play at the Bristol Psych Fest. Again, around 200 people were there.

I get something from both types of show. I'm under no illusion that Colossus playing at a 200-capacity venue is in any way connected with Kendrick Lamar playing to 16,000 people. You just must show the alternative. Give the option. Just because you're left wing or right wing, you own guns or you're a pacifist. If you're vegan, if you're religious. As much as you guide your children I don't think it's your place to force them to do or believe anything. What do I know? Both Stan and Freddie have been brought up vegetarian yet one day they may become big game hunters. They would have exercised their right to choose, for which I will applaud them. Then I will disown them. You're on your own now kids, the signed Faith No More albums will not be going to you when I die.

By 2015, and with the release of the two records, we were certainly keen on playing live and having fun with it. Not playing endless space jams that spun off aimlessly into the night. We'd done that for 12 years. You can hear our love for that way of playing but it's buried in amongst the tunes on the records. 'Hop' could be played forever; the structure is not too obvious. It's come from a love of jamming and playing as a band in a room. I think you can hear that.

Jon left the band after we toured these two records and before we began working on the next one. He wanted to focus on his solo music. It was a shame, but people can leave if they want. He released a solo record under the name Kreol Lovecall and toured Europe with Duke Garwood. This isn't a prison. I'm stuck in until the end though. I was once told you need to find a pebble with a hole in before you're allowed to leave the British coastal town of Hastings. It's the same for me with this band, only I don't know what I'm supposed to find before I can leave.

Jon was replaced by Roo Farthing, Tim's brother. As mentioned earlier Roo was part of the four piece we did almost 20 years back, The Young Hurlants. He also plays with Tim in the electronic/mystery/folk/occult duo Reigns. They've so far released four albums and created soundtracks for some BBC History documentaries. Their first two records were on Jonson Family. When we stopped the label they moved to Monotreme who did a way better job with them. Lovely vinyl versions, even some tour support. I played bass with them on a few of their live shows, alongside a drummer called Kunal Nandi. Kunal runs a label called SuperFi and plays bass in the power violence grindcore metal band Art Of Burning Water. Playing drums in Reigns was quite a sidestep for him. He managed with great ease. So, Jon went onwards and Roo came inwards. We were now a fifty-fifty Somerset-London mix.

We have done nothing with the new recordings. There's been talk, but nothing has happened. We've been entirely wrapped up in playing shows, they keep getting offered and we keep saying yes. We just played in Liverpool at The Wrong Fest, got home at 3am. This coming weekend we're playing at Sounds From The Other City Festival in Salford. We will get home at 3am. Leon has told us he can't do some of the upcoming dates so we're drafting in another new guitarist. Will Pearce from the Bristol band Pohl has stepped in. Roo and I have had a rehearsal down in Somerset with him, he has learned fifteen songs. He's done excellent work in learning them, he knows them better than us. I feel a little weird about it as he's really worked hard on the songs, as if they're proper songs. I can't get my head around us being a proper band. It's hard to think like that when you have a proper job and a proper family and a proper mortgage and a proper empty bank account. Will is in for the five upcoming Euro dates with Sumac and the Arctangent Festival in our home county of Somerset.

Today we drive to Stuttgart. I have my shorts on. We operate a strict 'no shorts on stage' policy. Rhys has broken this policy. It was in Italy and it was 100 degrees. He's the drummer so is working the hardest, fair enough. I have also broken this policy, at the Supernormal Festival and it was also very hot. Paul sort of has by being almost entirely naked in Istanbul, and Salford. Not tonight though, tonight we are to be serious and mature. It's a five-hour drive to Stuttgart. We never listen to music in the van, a couple of films have been watched but for the most part we talk. Time flies when you talk. It's not serious and deep but it can be, it's neither heavy or puerile but it can be. It just is.

The venue, JuHa West, is a youth centre. The promoter Florian Eymer also works there as a social worker. He is one of the nicest people. When he's sorting out the payment and I'm signing all the paperwork at the end of the night he lists all the bands who have played there or are going too. When you consider the venue holds 200 people and would feel uncomfortable when it gets filled then the list of bands who have played there is immense. Deafheaven, Gaslight Anthem, Agnostic Front, there's some heavy hitters. The show is probably our favourite of the tour, our playing has improved. We're tighter and all six of us have realised that we're incredibly lucky to be here and doing it. It shows. We're at ease.

Mr Inescapable is here with his wife. They both dance like there's no other soul there. The mainly black T-Shirt wearing audience shuffle back and forward taking inspiration. Mr Inescapable and his wife act as our Bez and help get the party going.

It's over too soon, as ever.

Sumac play and crush everyone. They are so damn heavy. During their first song I am showering. I have never showered straight after playing so tonight I had a total Jon Bon Jovi moment. While Sumac began cranking it out I was washing. The joy.

Standing around, Sumac have finished, coffee in my paw. A bearded man approaches. 'Are you Joe?'

I decide to tell the truth. 'Yes'.

This man was Malte, from a band who now don't exist called Black Shape of Nexus. They were one of seventy-six groups we got tracks from for a compilation we put together along with Andy at Riot Season. It was to raise funds for the Gate Community Centre in West London. Black Shape of Nexus are German. You may wonder why such a band, from Germany, would give a track for a random sounding cause.

There was also a man called Peter Kemp. He spent a lot of time at this particular community centre. He had learning difficulties but was looked after marvellously by a chap called Arlo Yates. Arlo realised Peter loved music and enjoyed writing. He started playing him records and a blog was set up for Peter to review records,* . The first record he wrote about was *RRR:*

"This record is by the Hey Colossus band and there were only 250 copies made of the record all painted differently. Hey

---

* http://peterkempsrecordreviews.blogspot.com

Colossus are from London and make noisy rock music with loads of guitars and heavy drumming and lots of screaming and shouting.

The record starts off with slow guitars and screaming ghostly voiced like from a horror film, this first track ends with some talking and then goes into the next song which sounds like they are swinging the guitars around their heads and banging them on the floor - it is a much louder track with more drumming and reminds me of a noisier Black Sabbath. The next song slows down a bit and has vocals which reminds me of witch-doctors making spells. Next song starts up with sounds like kids in nursery messing round then there's guitars and a lot of noisy feedback which sounds like a very very windy day and then the drums start banging and there are dark voices screaming ARRRRRRRRRRRRRRGHHHHH ARRRRRRRRRRGGGGGHHH and the guitars get louder before they all wind up very noisy but then calm down at the end.

First song on the second side is called Almeira, Spain but doesn't sound too Spanish it just sounds like noisy electric guitars but that's good. I have been to Spain, I liked it very much because it's nice and hot over there and we saw models made of sand and the beaches were lovely. The next song does sound a bit more Spanish as it starts with a guitar which sounds like a Spanish church bell and a deep voice which sounds like somebody praying and another voice which sounds like somebody dying. The song is very slow and lasts eight minutes long which is very long but I like it very much. The closing song is faster and has talking in it and what sounds like a priest in the background and then lots of loud guitars come in - it is a good way to finish the record.

Overall I think this was very good record by a brilliant band and I would give it ten out of ten."

And from here it spun out of control and went beyond Peter writing about Arlo's record collection. Bands and labels wanted Peter to write about their records. His writing was from the heart and direct, it wasn't informed by press releases. They were being sent music from round the world. Peter got ill. Arlo told us of this. It was decided to quickly raise some money for the centre, to give some thanks and love back. Within two weeks we had 76 songs. Sleaford Mods, Cosmic Dead, Gnod, Goat, Hard Skin, Acid Mothers Temple, Good Throb, The Wharves and many others donated music. The compilation was digitally released, we charged £5 and within a week had raised £1,300. The money was handed over and music equipment was bought for the centre.

What the man from Black Shape Of Nexus wanted to ask was whether Peter heard the compilation before he died. The answer to this is yes, he had heard it and he was really pleased about it.

Henry Blacker had a London show soon after the compilation came out, so we took a day off work and went to visit the centre in the afternoon. We set up our gear and for a few hours our gear was used by all in the centre. Tim, Roo and I didn't play any Henry Blacker tunes. I didn't play at all. There was rapping, dancing, all sorts of singing and various people played the drums and guitars. It was one of the best things we've done with music. Nothing beats unadulterated joy, nothing can disguise genuine warmth. Cynicism is for the tired and bored.

The van gets packed and we go to bed in the venue. Venues that have a room to sleep in are heaven on earth.

26

TOTAL DEFEAT
(Not on) The Guillotine
2017

The one that got away. By my reckoning we've had a good few that have got away, but this song did a proper runner. The recording sessions for *The Guillotine* took place over four long weekends, one at Dropout and three at Hackney Studios. Have you ever driven to Hackney from Somerset? I'm going on record to say it is the worst journey possible in Europe. We've played many shows there, I knew it was a grim one. Now we were recording there. God damn. I was so glad to be going there three times. The studio is great, the travel not so much. Coupled with the fact we stayed in South London while recording and the ten-mile journey at midnight took ninety minutes and the same again in the morning. I was tired of London. When Samuel Johnson said that boringly famous line, 'When a man is tired of London, he is tired of life', all those years ago he wasn't having to drive to Hackney in 2017. He was prancing around in the 18th Century, skipping over horse dump and waiting for football to be invented (probably).

The first session at Dropout was with Tim Cedar at the desk, and it was OK. We weren't entirely ready, but the main problem was the only toilet in the place was out of bounds. The flush was broken, it was blocked, and it was already very full. I can't put this in a polite way. It was piled high. 'Glastonbury day six' quantities. It stank. People did eventually stop putting more into it but sadly didn't stop pouring piss in. Each time more piss was added the stench was re-ignited. We couldn't go back to Dropout after this and to this day we haven't been back. The all-clear has never been given. We moved the session to Hackney. Instead of encountering the toilet in Camberwell I had to drive to Hackney. What he gives with one hand he takes with the other. We also switched to using Ben Turner to record the session. Tim did pop in a few times though. We fancied switching things, to keep it fresh. Ben is from Yeovil, Tim F and Roo both knew him from time's past.

When we record an album, almost certainly like when any band records an album, we aim to record more songs than we need. This gives us some choice. Dump the songs that suck, pick the best, or pick the songs that fit best together. There were four songs that didn't make the cut for *The Guillotine,* one of which we played live a few times. We opened the set for a few months with a song that was very rock, called 'Blue Fields'. It had a 'metal song done by Jesus Lizard' feel. It got dropped from the album, it didn't really fit. I personally wished we'd altered the structure slightly for the recording. The song I was most sad about, though, was 'Total Defeat'.

Tim F had the main idea. Him, Roo and I jammed it in Roo's loft then brought it to the others. It was turned into a song. It was quite poppy. A downbeat pop song. The main riff had the same time signature as 'Golden Brown' by The Stranglers. When you next hear that tune count out the rhythm of the opening 30 seconds, and again when that pattern comes back. The time signature rolls around like this: 3/4 – 3/4 – 3/4 – 4/4

We did the same on 'Total Defeat'. Not on purpose and of course not to the same skill level. It was very nice to play, and the overall feeling of the song was very different to a normal HC tune. It was folky in places, then straightened out on the chorus. It lasted three minutes. We worked hard on it in the studio, getting the feel right and all knowing exactly what we were doing. A problem kept coming back though, it sounded like someone was playing a wrong note. We analysed what was going on, stripping it all back, playing one guitar then another. We thought we'd dealt with it. It got recorded and we listened back. Once Paul had put his vocals on it was sounding excellent. They were arguably his best vocals from the new songs:

'Lining the streets with total defeat,
don't talk like you once thought you stood a chance here.'

When the rough mixes came through the issue became apparent again, we'd been blinded in the studio. Through big speakers everything sounded epic and perfect. We were taken away by the fact it's our band and we were playing. We'd stopped listening. At home, using the same crappy £9.99 headphones that dad spent hours listening to the *Cuckoo* rough mixes through, the muddled moments we thought we'd solved were clearly still unsolved. It was baffling, we'd all played the correct notes but together they were turning to mud. I went to the place everyone goes too when researching such issues, I went to social media. All sorts of folk chipped in, but here's Chris Summerlin, a man with some heavy guitar knowledge. Here he talks about the issues a band can have when many are involved and you're all downtuning.

"With tuning issues there's two things usually going on. Being out of tune is the most obvious. Even if the guitar is 'in tune' (i.e. the open strings read what they should on a tuner) the guitar itself won't necessarily intonate 'right'. The more stringed fretted instruments you have in the mix the more likelihood that one of them is going to be a little teeny bit out once you start fretting stuff. That's the one that you're going to hear as it'll make that 'wobble' you get when you tune one string against another. Add into this the heaviness that the person is playing the guitar with. The harder you hit the strings (especially detuned) the sharper they go on attack and no two people hit the strings the same. One of our Grey Hairs songs always sounds out of tune in the chorus as Amy tenses up, grabs the bass neck hard and bends the E string slightly as she twats it so it goes sharp. I have to bend my whole chord up a tad to make it sound right".

I asked the others about it. Paul said, "I remember liking it, thinking it should go on the record. Reading through the lyrics and thinking about it makes me really depressed now, though. For various reasons". Bob reckoned, "That song would have been a hit". I told you, Bob doesn't write much, I definitely intend to get to the bottom of that. Roo went into more detail, and pretty much confirms Chris's technical explanation:

"When we were first working that song out, the three of us in my attic, I remember thinking we had stumbled onto something really special. When we came to record it, I thought Paul's vocal was outstanding and it would be the best thing on the record. But the tuning did gnaw away at me. Most guitars don't really like being downtuned. On my guitar I can tune the bottom string to C and it can be perfectly in tune until you actually fret a note. The fifth fret might sound perfect but the

6th can be out. Multiply that by four guitars, each with their own unique tuning issue. When a song is so clean and simple it's always going to be a challenge. It's so much easier to get away with tuning inaccuracies when you're doing something loud. I remember really wanting the song on the record but knowing it wasn't quite right and that it hadn't turned out as well as it should have."

'Total Defeat' caused a fair bit of debate. We ended up dropping it *and* the three others leaving us with an eight-track LP. There was initial talk of all the recorded songs making up a 12-song double LP. Bands seem to be 80% email, 10% driving and 10% playing music nowadays. This period, mid to late 2017, we certainly did all three of these activities to the maximum.

Tim left soon after to concentrate on Reigns and writing. We played the shows to promote the record and he left. His last show being Lille as mentioned previously. The last song we played with him was 'Hot Grave' as an encore, an appropriate ending. Tim had spent 10 years with us. It had been a pleasure. His microphone soundcheck, for 10 years, always tickled. Gently speaking into the mic, 'One. Two. One Two'. Being nice and polite to the sound person. Then, out of nowhere Brian Blessed would appear. Brian Blessed meets Barney from Napalm Death. An enormous roar would pour out. The sound person would have to readjust their previous settings. Absolutely splendid memories.

There you go. That's what had happened. I still like listening to the song but we'd essentially downtuned it to death. Consequently, only seven people will ever hear it. The band and Ben. If I was being honest I'm not entirely sure how the song would have fitted soundwise on the record. It would have got out somehow though, as a seven-inch or compilation tune. As it stands it's buried deep like nuclear waste, or hopefully like the Dropout toilet.

I thought, to end this chapter, it'd be nice to speak to Ben. He was the long-suffering studio maestro for *The Guillotine.* We're also using him on the current record and I don't doubt will use him on into the future. He has a calm way about him. He's very organised in the studio and knows how to run the mixing desk.

Why, in your opinion, did this song – Total Defeat – not work?
"I think the song itself was good, easily good enough for the album. But the way Hey Colossus work, writing as we record, with that particular song being more vocal driven, we ended up with a great demo rather than a finished album track. We then could have gone and re-recorded it with a more traditional multi-track approach and probably had a great recording. But that's definitely not Hey Colossus's style. Which is one of the things I like about working with them. It's very exciting when the good stuff goes down. But there's also a much higher kill rate for tracks, like 'Total Defeat'. Also, the track may have been a step too far musically, the band evolved a bit on *The Guillotine.* And this track was probably at the extreme of some of the new elements being brought into the band."

How much do you step in when a band is struggling, or, in your opinion, not being very good?
"I tend to step in with drums sounds, swapping instruments and guitar tones if the band want me too. But if the band, like HC, have their own things going on, I stay well away. Like Rhys' snare. On paper it's completely wrong, the way it's tuned. But it works really well in the context of the band. So, if I jumped in

and tuned his snare like a typical rock snare, it'd suck.

Musically I try and keep my contributions/suggestions to just pointing out when things are good. Not letting a band or artist destroy their own track with pointless overdubs. Also, you sometimes need to let a band struggle for a while on their own and figure their own stuff out. I think producers can be way too keen to stick their ideas in. They end up making a good record, but not one the band recognises as them. My main aim is for the band to hear themselves coming out of the speakers. If we're really against the clock I might suggest something to get things moving.

I had a slight feeling 'Total Defeat' would either need a lot of work or might not make the album. I was new to working with the band and there was so much other good stuff going down I didn't think about it too much".

How do you find the way HC works, especially in comparison with other bands?

"Like I said before, I like working with HC because when you're recording ideas as they first come into focus it can be exciting and have a real magic to it. From playing in bands myself, I know the best few times you play a song can be when it's first written. And that's normally when HC are laying the track to 'tape', they've just got it coming together so it's fresh. Most bands have been thrashing a song out for weeks or even years by the time they hit the studio, so a lot of the initial excitement is gone.

Also, with HC we track all in the room with no headphones which has its challenges technically. Luckily they spend a fair bit of time writing so I have plenty of hours to move mics around, turn amps up and down etc. What you lose in flexibility come mix time you more than gain from all the stuff you get when everyone's gelling in a room together.

I tend to either like to record live, all in the room, no cans. Or build it from scratch, everything separate, to a click, more like a hip-hop track. Both have their up and down sides. It's more about how the band are comfortable working."

27

CALENTURE BOY
from The Guillotine
2017

Tim, Roo and I also make up the band Henry Blacker. We went through 2016 rehearsing both bands at the same time. We were booking a rehearsal for the three of us with no idea which band we were going to be working on. We would bring the ideas to the others. The others could reject them. The others could dig them. Unlike the song 'Total Defeat', this one, 'Calenture Boy', made the album.

It starts with just Roo, then Tim joins in. It's the quietest and mellowest song we've done. The two of them pick their way through some notes for a minute or so, Paul joins in on the vocals. It was a huge development for us to have the vocal so up front, so bare. We all come in after a couple of minutes and it has a heavy, relaxed feel. Bob's feedback precedes us all joining in, it all arrives with an ominous swell. The music was recorded late 2016, Elisa recorded some backing vocals on New Year's Day 2017. It was fun being up and recording at 9am on the first day of the new year. It had the feeling of the beginning of something more than just another year.

Around ten years previous Elisa was diagnosed with primary biliary cirrhosis (now called primary biliary cholangitis), PBC for short. It's an autoimmune illness that affects the liver. It is not caused by alcohol. I feel like I need to say this every time I ever mention it to someone. In fact, I believe it's why the name change happened as the word cirrhosis is so linked with alcohol destruction. It's a slowly progressing disease that over time kills off the bile ducts around the liver. She's tired a lot of the time and spends a lot of time laid up in bed. The other main symptoms are extreme itchiness, nausea and pain. We've been to hospitals from Newcastle to Plymouth. It will eventually end up with a liver transplant. Half the visits we have to hospitals seem to result in us discussing when this will be. The other half finds us looking at ways to halt the slide towards the inevitable. After recording the vocals on New Year's Day she spent almost two months in bed. This wasn't a result of getting up early on New Year's Day I don't think, it just happens this way occasionally. Backing vocals were laid on three of the album tracks.

Elisa had sung in bands before, her main band was called The Tony Head Experience. They were based in the village of Street in Somerset, which is where we live now. They'd released a few seven-inch's and a couple of flexi discs on their own label. This was the pre-internet, flexi discs were still a big deal. She'd also sang in John Parrish's band, Automatic Dlamini, whose alumni includes PJ Harvey. I'm always trying to get her to sing more. We all need to be pushed a little. As it stands Elisa is our merch person. She's a self-professed lover of talking so enjoys the chat that comes with people buying records and T-Shirts. It would be nice to get her singing onstage again. One day. I am slowly introducing the idea.

Paul's lyrics on *The Guillotine* are the best he's done to date. 'Calenture Boy' being no exception. The whole record had a Trump/Brexit, staring into the sun, wondering what the hell has happened feel too it. We weren't the only band doing this around this time. Gnod, also on Rocket, released a record in 2017 with arguably the most up-front album title of all time: *JUST SAY NO TO THE PSYCHO RIGHT-WING CAPITALIST FASCIST INDUSTRIAL DEATH MACHINE.* Yes, it has to be written in capital letters. The system was feeling rigged. All minorities were getting the rough end of the stick, getting blamed. A head scratching time. The country was split. Families who were all politically left or right weren't voting the same way. We hadn't been an outwardly political band before now, aside from how we acted. Paul's lyrics were supported by all of us. It was exciting listening to them when the recording was happening. You don't know what's being sung in rehearsals, lines and phrasings are being worked out. When they came back at us through the speakers we all knew he was doing good work:

"From alpha, to beta, to gamma, we're gone"

It seems best to let Paul speak here:

> "As much as I'd like songs to not be about one certain thing, there's a Threads-esque theme of world-ending events. Guess that's the image a lot of people turn to when looking for a hook to hang their intense uncertainty about life, especially as psychotic as things appear currently.
>
> But then, I finally got to use a couplet that I'd had written down for about seven years so it's not completely reactionary. Not saying which one.
>
> By the way, alpha, beta, gamma are the levels of radiation with which you can gauge the point of no return.
>
> There's good radiation as well of course, cancer treatment etc.
>
> Maybe it's a love song?"

When Elisa was working out the lyrics to add the backing vocals we didn't have the words to work with. One was misheard and sung incorrectly. It was altered forever to the new line, 'So sickening' became 'So sick of men'. It stuck. It worked. It summed up what all humans in 2017 should have been thinking. It was time for a change at the top. We all felt that men have had a fair crack of the whip for the previous *whole existence of time*. We can only hope.

We aren't the youth. We've for a long time not been the youth. But we are part of the majority, the people who aren't running the country. We can have a say, we can vote. We can be educated. A lot of politics come out through art, and art can influence. I would argue, when political histories get written, that the influence of politics in art gets overlooked. Personal politics, how you act in your everyday life can be seriously swayed by how your favourite band live their life. If they talk of left or right-wing ideals their audience will take heed. If they screen print their own T-Shirts, if they release their own records. If they interact directly with their audience, if they act like the audience isn't there. All these things can make someone behave in their own life in a certain way. Ultimately, personal politics is about creating a small version of how you'd like the whole world to be run. Set up your own show, police it yourself in the way you see fit. Release your own records, price them how you see fit. Start a band, don't rule out anyone from joining. Art is perceived by the viewer, music is listened too by the fan. They create their own story. They decide what the meaning of the work is. You can say what you want about what it means but it's in your actions where the ultimate truth will come.

As a live song 'Calenture' works sitting in the middle of the set. We don't have ballads. This isn't our 'Every Rose Has A Thorn' or 'Sweet Child O'Mine'. It is a mood changer though, it's slower, it has a structure with strict verses and choruses. It's a serious song. We treat it as such. If you're playing live for more than 30 minutes, it helps to have a tune that changes the mood. It's nice to let the person doing the lights press the *red light only* button. Let's bum people out. Let's have some swaying. Computer phones in the air, lights on. The boringly safe version of the lighters up, get some naked flames going, burn this place down, good times of yesteryear. This by the way does not happen at our gigs, unfortunately. It did happen at the Kendrick Lamar show that Freddie, Elisa and I went too though, and I will say it was very impressive. Even if it felt a little 'Muse'. I tried to find the light on my Nokia in time to join in. All the buttons are so worn out I stumbled at it like an old man trying to find the correct Emoticon to convey 'confused, help, winky fist bump'.

May 6th, 2017
We play the Old England pub in Bristol, part of the tour to spread the word of *The Guillotine*. Adam Reid in Bristol has put our last three or four shows on in my new nearby city. He goes under the moniker Cacophonous Sarcophagus. I've fallen in love with Bristol. You can walk it. It's filled with record shops and venues and a posh bridge designed by Brunel that costs one pound to traverse. We wanted to play a different venue to normal. Adam booked the Old England, a pub with a seventies crusty feel. You could imagine walking in and seeing Crass or being pounded by a gratifyingly large reggae sound system, £1.20 entrance fee, mohawk punks asleep in vomit on the floor. But today it's us and

a couple of bands we've asked to play alongside us, EUH! and the Dust Trio.

Over the year before this show, based out of Blackcat Records in Taunton, a group of likeminded souls had been meeting up and chatting and eating and playing music. The nights were called *Cani E Porci*. The main man behind it, Stef Giaccone, was Italian, and wanted food and music and talking to be as one. Trying to take back music. Trying to take control, attempting to reclaim it for what it was and what it should be. A thing for all that has nothing to do with the industry that has sprung up around it. Through the 1980s Stef was in a band called Franti who were all about social inclusion and not being tied down to a genre. He worked in Blackcat with the main man there, Phil Harding. The two of them chatted a lot. They chatted more than they sold records. I would spend hours in there, drinking tea and not buying records. Blackcat closed in the end. No idea why. Out of these *Cani E Porci* nights came the two bands who played with HC in Bristol. Euh! is Kek W and Wayne Rex, with Kek's homemade electronics cruising over the top of Wayne's spectacularly exciting jazz drum style. They began by playing shows to no one on wastelands around Yeovil. Dust Trio are aged from twenty to eighty. An ex-RAF pilot painted while twenty Walkman's were looped together, guitars, rhythm, saxophone. They weren't a trio.

The show at The Old England was free entrance, donations if you want. It was a Friday night and it was packed. It was exactly what the *Cani E Porci* nights were about. A big social evening for everyone. That at best would inspire and at worst would at least not cost anything. I think the high from this show lasted longer than any hangover gained.

28

KEEP IT OUT OF YOUR HEART
from The Making Of Junior Bonner
by the band Henry Blacker, 2018

Friday April 13th, 2018, I'm up at 5am for work. Someone has gone sick so as one card gets pulled out the whole house comes down. Three or four of us get moved to cover rounds. I end up on a delivery that takes longer with someone who's been drafted in from another office. I don't mind. It's my job. The hours are my hours. The person who's been drafted in doesn't know the round so it takes longer. On the plus side he's a VW fanatic so we talk about our mutual fascination with these machines. It does mean I won't get home to have thirty minutes of sleep before picking Tim and Roo up at 4pm to head to Plymouth.

Our new record is out today, *The Making Of Junior Bonner*. It's on Riot Season Records. It's our third LP for them and we can't believe how lucky we are that Andy at the label is still keen on releasing our records. I compare us to a band from America called Arcwelder. They aren't a popular band and they would possibly be the first to admit this. The label that releases their records is called Touch and Go. According to the band they send a finished record to the label and Corey Rusk, the main man there, listens to it, digs it, and says 'yes'. The band know they don't sell many. The label knows they don't sell many. Yet time after time Touch and Go releases Arcwelder records. The main man at Touch and Go just loves Arcwelder and that's all that matters. They have bands that probably sell ten times as many records. This is a key thing though. It's not about the sales, it's about the love. Whether Andy at Riot Season loves Henry Blacker I wouldn't like to say. But as we're on our third album with him and I doubt we do more than break even he can't hate us.

We get to Plymouth at 6.10pm. It's only two hours away. Down the A303 to Exeter, M5 for a couple of miles then onto the Devon Expressway to Plymouth. The roads in the South West are beautiful. The A303 is one of my favourite roads in the country, but god damn it gets busy around Stonehenge. Why can't everyone else find a different route and let us enjoy it on our own. We are the first people at the venue. It's a community space in a slightly rundown area of Plymouth opposite the now derelict Palace Theatre. You can buy the now derelict Palace Theatre for 'a few million' according to the couple drinking tea outside the hostel next to where we park. 'Laurel and Hardy's last show was there,' they say. We don't know whether to believe them. The building is incredible, all the original features are there. It's not been touched for twenty years so it's falling apart. At night it turns into a soup kitchen and did so on this night. On the floor outside the theatre are some brass plaques, one is of Stan and Ollie. Maybe we were told the truth, they were over in the UK in 1955, who knows.

The venue we're playing is called Union Corner, it's on Union Street. Other people start turning up, other band folk. Some people who want to come to the show are sniffing around. Daniel Leahy the promoter rolls in at 7pm. He has the keys to the space. According to the poster for the show the doors are open at 7pm. I guess this was a time guide for the bands to be able to get into the venue rather than for the punters to show up. Union Corner is a community space. Through the week they give out free soup in the daytime. I know they have African drumming sessions weekly as our new tea drinking friends told us it was 'terribly loud'.

The venue used to be a shop. You have standard shop windows staring straight out onto the street, staring straight at The Palace Theatre. There is no soundproofing. African drumming would definitely be heard by our tea-drinking friends. The space was saved by some pro-active locals, they knocked it into shape. Someone has provided a PA. The whole room has the feeling of utter righteousness. The venue costs £5 an hour to hire. It's a bring your own drinks venue. In the same room as the bands are playing there's a kitchen with a kettle, a fridge and a sink. A single toilet is the only other room. This is not a standard venue. I drink tea and coffee all night. I'm in heaven. If you run a venue, please put a kettle in it. Pretty please. Some tea bags, a jar of any coffee, some cups. You will win over many hearts.

I can't think of a better venue to play on the day our album is released. Release dates aren't important any more and have never really been important in our world. I would say 15-20 shops will stock a new Henry Blacker record, most of our sales will be online. Andy will do the most, which is good as he's put the most money in. We have been given 20 per cent of the press. 300 records have been printed so we have 60. We're not talking *Brothers In Arms* or *Thriller* numbers. Remember, we are Riot Season's Arcwelder.

'Keep It Out Of Your Heart' is my favourite song on the new record. It's as poppy as we've gone. We're a cross between noise rock and stoner rock, we're not ashamed of this. We're in our 40s and this was the music of our youth. The band started for three reasons, the first being Roo wanted to learn the drums. Our first rehearsal was the first time he'd ever played drums with a band. The second reason was that Tim brought a riff to an HC rehearsal and it was rejected as being too complicated (a couple of years later all HC songs were more complicated but in 2013 we were still a simple band, so the idea was shrugged off). On the long drive home we came up with Henry Blacker as a Plan B. The third was geography. The three of us live in Somerset, we rehearse 20 minutes from our homes. Having spent the last ten years driving three hours to rehearsal this was a dream.

We wrote and recorded the first record in secret, sent it to Riot Season and told Andy our plan. Release an album out of the blue as a new band and have the shows to back it up. Andy was into it. We played over 50 gigs in the first two years. Considering we had a combined age of 130, a combined number of wives of three, a combined number of kids of five, we also had jobs and played in another band, we did OK. The record was also released on Learning Curve in the US. Rainer Fronz who runs the label was somehow connected with Amphetamine Reptile, home on occasion to the Melvins, Helmet and many other seminal US noise rock bands. The music he released was similar in spirit to that fine labels work. We were chuffed as our plan had worked. Secret band dropping a new album out of the blue.

Our first show was in Bristol in a crypt. The venue had no toilet and no bar as it was a crypt. The sound was terrible due to the main fact that it was a crypt. The door into the room was four feet high and there was no PA, both these things were related undeniably to the traditional nature of a crypt. To empty yourself you had to go outside and round to the back of the venue. There's some stunning little lanes leading off left and right, it's an old city. Tucked behind churches and in amongst the olde-worlde Victorian setting you had to find somewhere quiet, praying no one walked around the corner. The stunning little lanes would have little rivers stinking and damping up the Dickensian setting. To be fair, these lanes were very probably full of little rivers in the 19th Century as well. There's nowhere that says Dickens wasn't checking out some sounds in a crypt and having to sneak off to find somewhere quiet in a lane. You only ever hear the good stuff about these characters. It felt nice to add some authenticity to the place.

The gig was decent. It was good to get off and running. We then played as much as possible over the next couple of years and recorded a second record, *Summer Tombs*. That came out in 2015. HC were very busy through 2015 to 2017 so Blacker went a little quiet, occasional shows and some rehearsals to slowly work on new things. In the summer of 2017 we recorded *The Making of Junior Bonner* and here we are, April 13th, 2018 in Plymouth with a new record.

Like The Crypt in Bristol, the Union Corner in Plymouth has a DIY feel. My favourite venues are all like this. Run by the community for the community. The places we play that are like this are almost always more welcoming. Music is a communal action. It should be brought back to this, it's an art form for everyone. It should be available for everyone to play and watch at a cost that is in no way prohibitive. If you want to spend £80 to see Radiohead or whoever, then go for it but be aware that it's that price because they hate you. They hate you having money instead of them. Their record label hates you. Their record label hates you having money for beans and tea bags.

Major bands on major labels now sign a contract called a '360 deal'. A 360 deal is new. It's come about because the music industry had utterly missed the boat on technology over the last twenty years. It was so happy fleecing you with CDs that cost tuppence to make yet could be sold for £15. It was so happy celebrating that epic crime that it missed what was happening. We started stealing music. We said: give us a break music industry, we only need one copy of *Revolver*, we only need one copy of *Tango in the Night*. The 360 deal came in. It's where the industry now has a piece of all the various pies, from music sales (digital and physical) to merchandise (T-Shirts, key rings, hats) and through to concert tickets (it's £80 to see Radiohead or whoever now? Yes. That's because Thom Yorke or whoever needs to eat but so does every hanger on in the industry). We're being told it's our fault the prices are so high. I say it's their fault. They didn't plan for the future. They were head in sand, nose in coke, genitals in other people's wives. They blew it, we pay for it.

Music should be for everyone and the way for that to happen is to educate everyone that paying £80 to see Radiohead or whoever is a choice. It's not something you have to do. You can pay £5 to see four bands at The Union Corner in Plymouth. You can bring your own drinks, you can meet people and start something new. You can create, or you can watch, but either way it's for you and it's not run by them. Do whatever with your money, but don't complain about paying £80 to see some men from Oxford or wherever. Vote with your heart and mind. By the way, I don't hate Radiohead. They seem decent people. They are used here as an example. There are many worse bands. Do you want my top five worst bands? Email me for them, I will go into detail.

When we play places like the Union Corner I feel alive with what can happen. I have a list of places throughout Europe that are like it. Whenever we book a tour or plan one-offs I hope and pray we hit up one or a few of them. A little list, from the last fifteen years, of places that are like it:

The Kirkgate Centre, Shipley

We've played this hall three times. Once as HB, twice as HC. They sell cups of tea and homemade cake. Golden Cabinet run the nights and each time we played we were on bills with bands and acts that were so enticingly varied (Karen Gwyer, Not Waving, Gnod) that people travelled, and the nights sold out. Put on by a crew of excellent souls that knew what people wanted, they sparked nationwide interest. I would even argue these Golden Cabinet nights were the most influential events put on in the UK from the last ten years. I've had people from Taunton to Ramsgate talking about them and taking heed. Things were being set up in places a long way from Shipley, itself a town not renowned for music nights, because of word of mouth chatter.

New River Studios, Manor House, London

HC have played here a couple of times. The first being the night of the general election in 2017, the night before we flew to Italy. The show was announced only a couple of weeks in advance as we'd played London only just before. The venue is in a rehearsal studio complex with a café and a radio station. It's on the outskirts of an industrial estate, around a mile from Manor House tube. It wasn't long ago that a venue like this, in a location such as this, would have struggled. Now though, as people are moving further out these places can pop up. An excellent spot. A couple of rooms to play live, all-day festivals happen here, bands rehearse, people eat. It's the way forward. Get away from the corporate grip, things don't have to be run in that fashion. They can be run in a way the works for the musicians and the community. Put back what you expect to get out. Top tip for bands, not related but similar: If you stay at someone's house then do the washing up, you're not in such a rush that you can't behave in a civilised manner. Put back what you expect to get out. Do your bit.

South Street Arts Centre, Reading
Both HC and HB have played this place twice. Both bands have played their own shows there and both have played the Double Dot Bash. The DDB is a yearly festival partly run by the characters from Workin' Man Noise Unit. They are a Riot Season band who we love above and beyond pretty much any other UK band. They have something about them. A swing. A smile. Tunes. They bring it live. South Street Arts Centre is a tidy venue in a town 30 miles from London, which because of this location bands often avoid playing. It's been a battle keeping this place open, but it seems stable now. It has two rooms and a couple of bars. For the most part it has theatrical plays and local community action. It also has nights where local promoters can hire it. It's not a standard venue. You can get a cup of tea or coffee. I know, I go on about this, but how hard is it to be able to provide this as an option? Not every band wants European strength lagers. A lovely venue that the people of Reading should be proud of.

The 1in12 Club, Bradford
HC has played here twice, once with Pharaoh Overlord and once as part of an all-day festival. Arguably the go-to venue for punks in the UK. It used to be a squat then gained some level of legality. It was begun in 1981 by a local anarchist collective and is the ultimate social space. It's been at its current location since 1988.

It's a member's club, the members have weekly meetings. Events are discussed and agreed upon. It's the ultimate punk venue in the country and I don't have much more to say. Check it out if you don't know it. It's the bar for all other venues to aim for.

Magasin4, Brussels

We've played here so often that when we walk into the venue through the back door, which is right next to the river, it's like we've never been away. It's huge. We may play it one day and Napalm Death will be on the next night, Suicidal Tendencies the night after that. Its capacity is 500. Once you arrive, early afternoon, you don't leave until the next day. There's a kitchen where volunteers provide food. There's sleeping for twenty or so people, there's a shower. You have no need to leave. The night runs on for hours after the bands finish with regulars drinking and new faces drinking and the promoter drinking and the bands drinking. Someone takes control of the playlist and has it pumping through the venue's speakers. Going to bed is fine. Waking up at 4am to go to the toilet you have to walk through the venue which is either ghostly and empty or still buzzing with drinkers depending on the night. It's the best venue in Europe. Make it your ambition to play at M4 in Brussels.

We've played other places that are similar, The Commonplace in Leeds, Islington Mill in Salford and Ramsgate Music Hall. There are other spots that I'd love to play one day, London's DIY space and Cathays Youth and Community Centre in Cardiff. You can pick and choose where to play, but if possible try one or two of these. They undoubtedly broadened my mind, they may yours too.

The subject matter of 'Keep It Out Of Your Heart' along with the music touch me in a way that I find it hard to play. We have a song called 'Summer Tombs' (from the album of the same name) that I find so wrenching that I barely like playing it at all. With 'KIOOYH' though it's about the media, it's about manipulation:

> "It will osmotically seep in, the sewage that you choose to wallow in, devolving even as we speak, forgetting what or even how to think. Keep it out of your heart, keep it out of your mind and your mouth. It is persuasively laid out, voicing things you've never thought about, how all those children washed up dead, bought this down upon their heads. Keep it out of your heart, keep it out of your mind and your mouth. Now your mind is in their hands, when they palpate it you just have to act, and anonymously threaten death to people that you have not even met. Keep it out of your heart, keep it out of your mind and your mouth. With every page you turn a frost is setting in, your blood runs slow and cold you are fossilizing, throw down your barricades and remember what you were, and you can be again if you just hold your nerve."

– Tim Farthing

Tim's lyric writing is second-to-none. One day this will be flagged up and the world will wonder why people ever gave two hoots about him from Elbow (Elbow bloke) or him from Bob Dylan's band (I can't remember his name) or anyone else. He puts serious time into writing. The three albums we've released all have the lyrics printed on the back. He wasn't keen. I forced it through like a bully. They need to be read by as many people as possible. It's the same with the artwork. On this record Roo painted the sleeve and it's so accurate a depiction of Peckinpah and McQueen, it's uncanny. They're discussing a take or their retirement or their families. Whichever. The sleeve is black and white, we're middle-aged men still going at it and the title of the record and the artwork and the lyrics all scream this.

The song is tricky to play. There are some changes that need us all to stare at our fretboards like we've never seen them before. There's a lot of melody in the song. We don't always have a lot of melody in our songs, but with age we've begun to appreciate that melodies are timeless. It can't all be about smashing your way through to the point. Through all three of the records the words cover politics and health as recurring themes. Some of the politics are personal, some are Westminster. Either way something is always being said. In HC Paul is the lyric writer, he covers similar ground. On *The Guillotine* he came into his own with the lyrics, it was a massive step up. When your one of the grunts at the back, plonking on your bass, the front person is leading the charge. When the front person has something to say and you totally believe in it you can 100 per cent join in the rally. The playing improves, the whole band moves with a swing that is to the same beat.

When you match up the lyrics with playing shows like the one on April 13th in Plymouth at Union Corner. When on the other side of the road there's a soup kitchen running in a beautiful old run-down theatre. When 100 people show up and it feels like a collective of souls all part of a community action. When respect is shown to all in attendance and the kettle is constantly boiling. When everyone can see the whites of each other's eyes and the music is blasting right up close, you wonder why anyone would pay £80 to see Radiohead or whoever. I don't care about Radiohead, and not because I don't like them. Musically they're fine. In 1992 I was at college in Buckinghamshire, being taught by Mr Lake from Zounds, and there was a record shop called Track Records in Chesham. Radiohead's record label was essentially giving away the band's first two twelve-inch's, *The Drill* EP and *Creep*. No one was interested. They were 50p and Track Records had piles and piles of them. I bought one of each. How could I resist. Radiohead's record label forced that band on people. I don't care if they went and experimented and created new stuff later on. Ask anyone on Warp Records if they thought Radiohead were pushing new sounds. People are being manipulated into liking these bands. It's not just Radiohead, it's most of them. We're being told to like them; the whole industry is a marketing sham and we're being sold fakes. As Tim's lyrics say, "It will osmotically seep in…Keep it out of your heart, keep it out of your mind". We are manipulated into thinking we like things and then we go and buy the things. We are drones. We follow the adverts. We follow the radio. We follow YouTube's algorithms. Maybe I really don't like Radiohead?

On the drive home as midnight passed it turned into my forty-forth birthday, April 14th, 2018. Nothing was said of course. We bought a cheese and onion pasty from the services and drove across Blackdown Hills on the A303. The fog came down and slowed us to twenty-five miles-an-hour. No one else was on the road. The van lights were getting lost, full beam made it worse. We got to Roo's at 2am, Tim was dropped off at Podimore Services where his car was parked at 2.30. I got home around 3am and set the alarm for 5am. I was back in work for 6am and delivering mail around a new Prince Charles-approved estate up the top of Shepton Mallet. There's no shop or school or play area. It's houses upon houses, with roads that are too tight, with too many cars and tiny gardens. This is the future; we need housing, so we build houses. No amenities within walking distance. The Tesco in Shepton is enough for everyone, get in your car and go shopping.

Henry Blacker head off for four shows in Europe with the Brighton band Lower Slaughter. It's only the third time we have been across the water. The first time we played three shows and on the second trip we played just the once. In reality we've never really been over. Lower Slaughter have never been at all. They've just released their first record. It's a rager. 6Music have been playing it a lot and they've started to be added to bigger festival bills. They are younger than us. Much younger.

Day one, April 18th 2018, Paris
Up at 4.30am. Elisa is coming. We both get into the van and drive around Somerset picking up first Roo, then Tim. We meet with LS at our secret parking spot in Caterham, just south of Croydon, a mile or two north of the M25. This is where HC leave vehicles when we go abroad, it's South of London. The London types can meet us there, it means we don't have to drive into the city, it means we don't have to lose hours of our life on the South Circular. Today it's Henry Blacker's secret parking spot. To the ferry then onto Paris. We get to the venue at 5.30pm. It's called Instantes Chavires and it's on the outskirts. We've never played anywhere near the centre of Paris and it's not until we drive out of the city on day two do we get a glimpse of the Eiffel Tower. This is the first time I've ever seen it, having played Paris around 10 times now.

   Our friends Victor and Antoine are putting the show on. We soundcheck and try 'Keep It Out Of Your Heart', it doesn't sound exactly right. The recorded version is so nice. Through time this has happened, recorded versions being impossible to capture live. Very frustrating. The first band are called Grand Final, a duo. Doris has an excellent voice and can play the hell out of the guitar. They are a duo and we're all totally into them. They have an Earth meets Breeders feel. We both play. There's around 40 people in. The place holds three times that but we're happy, we don't expect any more and we're grateful anyone shows up. This comes back to bite us on day two, but for now we're happy. We head back to either Antoine's (Lower Slaughter go to his, stay up drinking and have a whale of a youthful time) or Victor's (we head to his and coo over his cat, Igloo, and admire his vast and varied record collection).

Day two, April 19th 2018, Rouen
Victor loves cooking. We awake to the smell of roasting vegetables and the sound of a droney, chimey record. (I meant to ask Victor what this record was, I will do next time we meet). LS turn up and we have lunch in the sun, a barbeque in Paris. If this isn't a perfect reason for travelling over the continent I don't know what is. It's the hottest April day for a hundred years, or the hottest April day on record, or something like that. Every day is the hottest or coldest or windiest or dampest day on record. Every city has the tallest this and the smallest that. So many records are broken all the time. How can anyone keep up? We were heading for a classic promoter excuse based on today's newly broken record.

It was a short drive to Rouen, a couple of hours directly north. The optimism in the van was peaking at around eighty-three per cent. We get to Rouen early and take a stroll around the most perfect and beautiful European city. Well-aged buildings overlooking bustling squares. Tables and chairs spilling out of sweet looking food and drink emporiums. The churches and the cathedral are picture book perfect. The people of France look straight out of fashion magazines or Kanye West videos. We look like the 'after' photographs of a particularly lengthy and gruelling fruit and veg drought. I'm not sure the people of the UK realise how we stack up in the order of things in Europe. Our island is insignificant, we are unimportant. Not all the maps of the world have us at the centre. We go to the venue. We're playing in the basement, it looks like it was once a wine storage room. It looks like it would hold fifty people at a push. Our optimism remained in the early eighties per cent. The show started on time and no one came. Not a soul. We played to each other. Jordan, the promoter, slouched about the place and was verging on tears all night. His gloomy mood was tough to take but being cynical and old we found a vast amount of gallows humour in the evening. Maybe, at tops, five people paid to get in, but it was more than likely that he let them in for nothing. It turned out all his shows recently had been dead rubbers. There were thousands of people in the streets of Rouen. A fair few that looked like they'd be into a night of downtuned rock. But they all stayed outside in the sun, drinking into the night, having an excellent time.

At this show we did not play 'Keep It Out Of Your Heart'. Even to an empty room we didn't risk it. The ghosts of Rouen's past may have judged us.

We had a long day coming so we all wanted to sleep in the same accommodation. We wanted to get away early the following morning. The only way to do this is to all be in the same place. A mistake. I drove the van through the streets to get to the house we were staying at, our host was in the front seat with us. We climbed the stairs to his abode, avoiding the hole in the floor, avoiding the damp patch by the front door. 'Do you mind snakes?' was uttered as we walked through the door. A very long and lively snake was awake in its glass walled home.

The house was over three floors. One room on each floor, each room around the size of two double beds. A close mixture of step ladder-spiral staircase took you from floor to floor. The house felt like a converted lift shaft. It looked like Escher's House Of Stairs. We filed in, one after another, passed the snake to the first set of stairs. Down them to a floor with the toilet and kitchen, both tiny. Then down again to the lower level. We could all fit in that room, those of us who suffered from claustrophobia began sweating. Maybe we would be buried in this room. Maybe we will die tonight. Maybe we'll finally start selling some records, on the back of our mysterious disappearance.

To confirm: We are always grateful when someone lends us a floor for the night. But this chap should have said, 'I don't think I have the room for eight people'. He should have said, 'I may be able to fit two people'. What he actually said was, 'I will sleep on the roof', and he did. Tim went back to the van and lay awake all night. Roo lay all night next to the snake that was trying to get at him. Lower Slaughter slept in the room at the bottom, next to a door that opened onto a brick wall. Elisa and I slept next to Roo. We were grateful for the floor to sleep on, we were grateful to leave. It was a long drive to Lyon, back past Paris and five more hours south. The tour routing was flawed.

Day three, April 20th 2018, Lyon
I wanted to go back to Lyon as we'd been there three weeks ago with HC. We'd played on a boat and I'd left my coat at the venue.

The van optimism level was fluctuating somewhat after we'd taken a battering in Rouen. A night to remember for many of the wrong reasons. It took forever to drive south. LS's Jon and I took turns to drive. I did the first chunk taking us out of Rouen and half the journey south. This turned out to be a blessing as to get to the venue in Lyon you have to drive 100 yards *up steps* through a large crowd of drinking Lyon-ites. If you've ever driven a Mercedes Sprinter with eight people and full backline up 100 yards worth of steps, you'll be familiar with the smell of a clutch burning out. You'll also be familiar with the stare of a few hundred people as you do it. I was glad Jon did this.

It was a free show, many people stayed outside in the glorious unseasonal heat but enough came in to make it a good night. I think both bands played their best shows. We didn't play 'Keep It Out Of Your Heart'. We will *never* play this song. It has such a different feel to all our others and arguably comes over a little too fiddly. It doesn't fit in our set. If we played it no one would question it. Yet we still don't play it. I think it will be forever lost in the middle of an album that will be owned by 300 people. I dream that one day Ben Wheatley, or a film director like Ben Wheatley, will hear it and put it in one of his movies. We still won't play it live but it'll begin to reach an audience that may find a crumb of comfort in its lyrics. Ben, the promoter, gave me my coat back. We slept in the same apartment we slept in three weeks ago, we parked in the same spot, we went to the same local supermarket, we began the vast drive north to Liege.

Day four, April 21st 2018, Liege
Another mammoth drive, seven hours with a couple of breaks. We arrive just as Brentford take a 2-1 lead into the final 10 minutes

against QPR. Barney in Lower Slaughter is also a Brentford fan. He has a computer phone and keeps the updates coming. I first met Barney when he was eleven years old. I'd got to know Colin Wakefield, his dad. He ran a record shop in Brighton called Edgeworld. I spoke to him when working at Vital as part of the telesales team. We got friendly and started occasionally meeting up at the football. We bonded over music and football. Colin also puts shows on in Brighton under the Tatty Seaside Town banner. Up to now, April 2018, we pretty much only play shows for Colin in Brighton, both HC and HB. I believe in sticking with those that are close if possible. Fight and win or fight and fail with the same folk. Build it together. Create a unity in each town and city you travel too. It's the same in London with Anthony Chalmers at Baba Yaga's Hut; Bristol with Adam Reid at Cacophonous Sarcophagus; Sammy Powell in Manchester at Beauty Witch; Chris Summerlin, Neil Johnson and Matt Newnham from Damn You! in Nottingham...etc, etc. These hero-gluttons are dotted everywhere and are doing god's work.

The show in Liege is a festival over two stages. We arrive as the band before Lower Slaughter start. They are a noise rock band, and all is going well until the bass player jumps into the crowd and starts thrashing about hitting a woman at the front. Bands do this sometimes. Male bands. They feel the need to act like they're losing it, maaaaan. I blame David Yow of the Jesus Lizard or D'Arby Crash or any of the frontmen who really were losing it. So many bands nowadays have frontmen who are faking being 'out there'. Eyes rolling in their head, falling over. Then when they get off the stage they're totally straight, go for a cup of tea and put their slippers on. Men, if you're not wasted don't act it. You look dumb. This thrashing bass player was a fool, he got told he was.

By this point Brentford had held on to their lead and the play-offs were looking weirdly possible. I like football, but I also really hate it. Modern football is not what I got into, but I can't help loving the team I support. Stan and Freddie do not like football. I will never encourage them to get into it as I wouldn't like it if I was a teenager nowadays.

Both us and Lower Slaughter struggle a little at this show, we play OK, but the local bands are getting all the love and attendance and while we play the crowds don't flock. Am I paranoid, does Belgium hate England? I wouldn't blame them. The food is lovely, the people putting the show on are great, the crowds are there but not for us. We stay in a Formula One Hotel on the outskirts of town. Don't book a Formula One hotel if you're thinking of impressing a partner, they are totally fine for grotty bands but not for romancing.

Day five, April 22nd 2018

We drive home. We leave Liege at 9am and get home to Somerset at 9pm. I put the kettle on and say hello to Stan and Freddie. They are now old enough to stay at home alone when Elisa and I head off to do these things. I think they love it. Stan was born when I was twenty-six, Freddie when I was twenty-eight. At the time I thought I was old to be having children, but now I'm forty-four and they are eighteen and sixteen I've reached the age where I think age doesn't matter. It really doesn't. With great age comes great wisdom and unpredictable back pain, terrible wind and the need for more sleep. And, of course, the requirement to make odd noises when getting up and sitting down.

Name a good live album.

There's around three in total. I'm going for *Crying Your Knife Away* by Guided By Voices and UFO's *Strangers In The Night.* OK, maybe there's only two. A lot of people like that Thin Lizzy one, I'm on the fence. I used to listen to *Live After Death,* Iron Maiden's 1985 effort, back when I was fourteen. I wonder if that's any good now.

With that in mind we thought it'd be a flawless idea to release our own effort. 300 pressed on vinyl, hopefully in time for our 15th anniversary show, July 2018. It will happen at The Moth Club in Hackney. Back into Hackney. The journey from hell for anyone coming from anywhere outside of Hackney, especially those travelling from the South West of England. I may have mentioned this already. I'd happily repeat it forever.

It was recorded straight to the desk at the Brussels show on our late 2016 Euro tour with Part Chimp. This means that all the mics used on the stage, the ones making the music be audible at the back of the venue by forcing all the sound through the big speakers (the PA), were also run into a recording facility within the mixing desk. A month or so later the venue sent us the files, then we got Johnny Chimp to master it. Paying him in *the usual way.*

Here's more on Magasin 4 from the insert that came with the record:

Magasin 4 is the jewel in the crown. It is the venue that all venues should aspire to. It has battled with the Brussels Council to remain open while around it gets built up. The cities are expanding, people are moving to areas that were before just dockyards or industrial lands. People want to live in converted warehouses, hang a guitar on the wall, impress their fellow office workers with their gritty new life. People want to move into farms, they want to sell the land and convert the working farm into a five-bedroom dream home. White collar in, blue collar out. Get rid of the previous ways, the new ways are cleaner. Magasin 4 has stood its ground while across the river folk move in and complain about the noise. They look across the water and see and hear what was there before them and they don't like it. It ruins their perfect dream, Vice magazine-inspired, grimey life. You do not move next to a church and complain about the bell ringing, you should not move somewhere and complain about existing things. Strict curfews and polite responses have kept the venue alive. You get treated beautifully, you get fed an evening meal and breakfast. You sleep in the venue. It is a haven for touring bands. Support venues such as this, they make things possible. This record was recorded direct to the mixing desk. The mixing desk, the lights, the stage and the organisation at Magasin 4 is stadium quality. This venue is run by volunteers.

I spend a lot of time analysing the live performance. The art of it. The skill needed. The point of it. What everyone gets out of it. Why the band feel they are important enough to be up there. Why people pay money to see the band. I over think it. When I was fifteen and reading *Kerrang* the singer from The Almighty, a UK rock band, was asked about what to do when playing live. 'Attack the front of the stage' was his reply. This turned me off so much I've spent twenty-five years doing exactly not that. That feels too *us vs them*. I prefer everyone to be in it together. When I watch a heavy band and they're at the front of the stage being total rock I get turned off. This is a little odd as I really do like heavy music. I think though that the heavy bands I like are all a little soppy inside, and I like that. They all seem a little more sensitive to the idea of the room being as one. Even AC/DC. Their main players (bass, drums, rhythm guitar) all stay at the back keeping out the way while Angus fannies around like he's lost his door keys for two hours. The idea of destroying a room, of crushing the crowd, seems so wrong. It should be about bringing everyone in. This is how I think. We play a lot of shows with bands who like to crush and kill and kick much arse. I admire them. I admire their seemingly unapologetic need to look tough and mean. It's hard for me to not picture the (comedy) band Bad News when they're asked to 'turn to the camera and look mean'. But still, I admire them in the same way I admire people who enjoy having their picture taken or like public speaking. Neither of those things are for me but I like looking at a good photo and a good talking person can be quite inspirational.

Before playing, if I'm sitting around on my own, I have a little think about what the hell it's all about. I don't think I have any other answer other than I enjoy it. I want other people to enjoy it. I want the night to be a worthwhile evening. I want everyone who's there to go away from it thinking positively about something.

It could be the music they've just heard, but it could equally be about going home and doing something themselves. Or maybe they just had a good time drinking with some friends and it was soundtracked by us and the other bands who played. I have no idea. The last few years has seen a more mixed audience, we used to get 99% men (87% with beards), we're now more like 72% men (36% with beards) and up to 28% women. We dream of a day when it's 50 (20% beards)/50.

The studio version of 'Black and Gold' is of course from the *In Black and Gold* record from 2015. Since it came out we've played it at every show without fail. The opening chords, originally played by Jon and now performed by Roo, bring a small amount of muffled recognition from the crowd. Not like Bon Jovi starting up 'Livin' On a Prayer', or when Anal Cunt tear into their seminal work 'You Quit Doing Heroin, You Pussy', but it does get a murmur of optimism from the crowd. We like going back to the same towns. Places where you start off playing to five people, then 15, then 30. Each time you go back you feel you're making new friends. Word of mouth works wonders. Constantly going back can feel like you're stuck in a loop, I've lost count of the times we've played Paris. We love playing Paris but we've played in some quiet venues there that over time have been getting more populated. It's such a cliché, but if you keep going back you do eventually win people round. When we were last in Paris and Roo played the opening chords to this tune I pretty much had a flashback, a life in front of eyes moment, remembering all the empty rooms. Again, we're not Bon Jovi, there wasn't 10,000 people there. There was 120 in a room that pretty much only holds 120 people, in the back of a restaurant. But on the back of no press or advertising or radio or any promotion other than social media it did feel like a small victory.

I feel like I'm constantly saying to anyone who will listen: there's two music industries. I have no real idea what people who aren't involved in this think, but I have a pretty good idea. They will possibly never understand the size of the work we put in against the almost no financial reward. If I try and explain it to someone, a fellow postman, someone at the football, they look at me like I'm the mad one. I am a broken record, I realise. It's this or fishing.

We released a live record to thank people for coming to the shows. We've pressed it ourselves. We're charging £10 for it, which in this era is tantamount to treason. Records are hitting the £20 mark nowadays. The Brexit vote screwed the pound and virtually all vinyl is currently pressed in Europe. The prices may not have gone up in Europe, but the pound went down so you have to pay more to get the previous equivalent. Seeing as this record cost us nothing to make due to it being recorded straight to the mixing desk we can keep the price low. If you want the finances, here they are:

It was £1200 for 300 records, in proper sleeves, with printed labels. We used a broker to press the record rather than going direct to the pressing plant. It's most common to do it this way. When we started Jonson Family in 1998 we went direct to the pressing plant. Now though, brokers have been set up all over the world and they can get reasonable deals as they put so much work towards the pressing plant.

That's it. If we sell 120 we break even. That's how we looked at it.

If this was a proper studio album the costs would be different as the recording prices would need to be taken into account. *The Guillotine* cost us almost £2000 to record, for example. Which, by the way, was the most we'd ever spent on a record by a long distance. We would also press a fair few more than 300. We know the audience for a live album is different to a studio album. If this was a proper studio record we'd try and get some press or radio. You can either do this yourself and send it to websites, magazines and radio presenters you think may like it. Or you can pay someone else to do it, a radio plugger or a press PR company. They vary from a couple of hundred pounds (if you're a small new band) up to over many thousands (if you're Muse). You may get more press and radio this way. You may not. There are no guarantees. You can pay for advertising, a banner ad on a website (a small amount of money, depending on the site) or you can put massive posters around the London Underground (£4-5000 at the most basic rate). If you wonder why certain bands become popular the answer may lie in the vast sums of cash poured into promotion. For our live record we're doing none of this. It's a live record, the only people interested will be the people who already like the band.

Not all record labels pay money to get press. Andy Smith at Riot Season hasn't done for the Henry Blacker records and didn't for the recent HC reissues (*RRR* was re-pressed on vinyl and *Happy Birthday* was finally given the vinyl treatment, nine years after the CD). Neither would have been worth it for him; we got about four online reviews for the recent Henry Blacker album. As before and as it will always be, we rely on word of mouth. We rely on Riot Season having loyal customers. We rely on the record being good enough to reach people. We play shows and sell them. They all go one way or another. There's a couple of hundred people who dig the band enough to buy a physical item. I have no idea about digital sales, I should pay more attention to this. If you don't have a PR person you normally don't get many reviews. There are so many releases nowadays. It probably helps magazines and websites to have a PR person point them in the direction of things. They can act like a guide through the crappy release infested waters, get them to the pearls. Or so they think. I believe that if you think you're a good music journalist you wouldn't just rely on the PR person, you'd dive for pearls yourself. The best do this, the worst rewrite press releases and claim them as their own.

With a song like 'Black and Gold', three years after its original release, our playing has improved. We're more confident with it. It's only natural, despite the line up being different from when the studio version was released. We probably play it faster, maybe heavier. If it's not getting better, or at least as good, why carry on playing it? We don't mind if it goes off piste. The other songs on the live record have all been previously released, they're all better now. It's for this reason we weren't against a live album, even if there's (apparently) only been two good live records ever (it has occurred to me that MC5's *Kick out the Jams* is no slouch). Some people have even asked for a live record. Some people. Maybe some people like live records, despite their grim hit rate.

We hope the live record turns up in time for the show.

Five date European tour, May 2018
Part F: Thursday May 31st

05:30. Time to get up and get the coffee pot on, start up the toaster, make some sandwiches.

06:25. We leave Stuttgart. Out of the venue's car park and up the winding roads leading out of this lovely city. The sun is climbing up the sky. There are no souls around, the roads are empty. Houses in Germany, Belgium, Holland are so beautiful. They are different. The atmosphere on mainland Europe is more chilled. We have fallen in love with the idea of moving to a European city. We hit the motorway. We know the day we're heading into. It's been worth it.

13:40. We make it to Calais. It's been a mammoth journey, around 750km. I am strict with the stops. Normally when we stop we're looking at thirty-plus minutes of wandering around the shop, the toilet, the smoking break, the fuelling up. Today I keep it to no more than 10 minutes. No loitering. We only stop twice, once after two hours and once at five hours. We had hoped to catch an earlier ferry, and we do. We're put on the 14:20, which is 40 minutes late as there's fog over the Channel. We're good with this. The ferry we were booked on was at 17:55 so we've shaved off three hours. Nothing beats the feeling of clawing back your life like this.

15:00. Our ferry departs Calais. Some of us eat, some of us pick up some wine in duty free. We all sit in the food court, talking and drifting off to sleep.

16:50. The South East dwellers are dropped off in Caterham, just inside the M25, extreme South London, our secret parking spot. Rhys drives Paul home, Bob heads off to catch the train back to Watford. See you all in two weeks for rehearsal. Will, Roo, Elisa and I head to Bristol. There's an amber warning regarding heavy rain in the South West. The weather has been stunning over the last five days. The traffic has been non-existent, all our journeys have been trouble-free. Now back in the UK we hit the M25 and it's jammed up to the eyeballs. It's pouring with rain and to top it off our windscreen wipers go crazy and start attacking each other. The rubber blades are too long, the two wipers get caught up in each other's tentacles. One dies. The other stutters on and off. It's like we're in the Bluesmobile and Jake is wiping his side so he can see through the murk while Elwood, the driver, is staring hopelessly through a rain splattered screen. On the busiest road in Europe. During rush hour. As the side door lets water through and into the rear. *No worries.* Welcome back to England.

20:31. Finally arrive at the van hire company in Bristol. We're to drop the van off, leaving the keys in a drop box. Switch the amps and drums and everything else into my smaller van and head home. But. We've lost my van keys. We can't find them. They are nowhere. We cannot remember what we did with them. Did I keep them? Did Elisa? It's been a long day, I sense it's not over yet. The four of us climb back into the hire van and head to Will's. We're going to have to drive down into Somerset, to our house a little over an hour away, to get the spare set of keys for my van. Roo will be able to go home from mine as his car is there. I'm undecided about what to do. Should I go to bed and deal with it in the morning as the van has to be back by 10am or should I deal with it tonight so it's done and I can sleep all day tomorrow. It's already been a marathon of a day.

21:09. Drop Will off, he lives on the east side of Bristol. He's done well on these dates, played well and has fitted right in.

22:20. We're home, in the hire van. Roo takes his guitars and amp. His pedal and lead box is missing. We may have left it in Stuttgart, it may have been stolen, Sumac may accidentally have it. Frustrating. I will look into this tomorrow*. Elisa's not keen on me driving back to Bristol. I grab Stan, get him to put some shoes on. He can come with me, he can talk, he can keep me awake.

23:01. To my dad's, the gear needs to be stored. Stan and I get it out the hire van and into his garage. Dad is well. He's been popping in to check on Stan and Freddie through the week. All has been good. Our sons are growing up, they are maturing, they can feed themselves.

00:04. Back up to Bristol to swap vans, for a second time. This time with the spare key. Stan and I drive home, an hour south. The roads are empty, I think it was the right thing to do. Get it sorted. No morning rush hour traffic. The fog is crawling over Somerset, we're listening to Tago Mago by Can, Stan and I are chatting.

01:23. Home. I climb into bed, finally. It's been a run of shows that will live in our memories. 3023km of driving that has tied together the stages, promoters, accommodation, people, food and venues that have proved the existence of a higher being.

---

* Update on Roo's pedal and lead box. Sumac had accidentally packed it. I received a message from their driver a week after we got back. The box was in the Czech Republic with the van hire company. I spoke with them and they sent it back to us, via UPS, at a cost of 48 euros. It was going to cost £350 to replace everything.

We don't play new songs to anyone. They stay under wraps until fully finished. Even when we think they're finished there's another tweak, a vocal addition, whatever. Hidden away they remain. Despite this, I played a couple of the new tunes as rough as they are to Elisa. Headphones on. House empty. I padded her down in case she was wearing a wire, had any recording equipment, was streaming it live to YouTube. She was really upset when Tim left after *The Guillotine*. I think she was worried that would be the end of the band. That Roo (as Tim's brother) would also jump ship and I would spiral into a never-ending deep depression. It is the thing I do with my spare time, I do nothing else. I may go to the occasional gig in Bristol but that's it. I used to go to football matches, I used to go to pubs. I made a choice, and this is it. Family. Work. Music. Sometimes I feel embarrassed that I so obviously have made this choice. There's great shame attached to nailing your colours to a mast. In the twenty-first-century the way to be is aloof and have a clear and apparent indifferent attitude. Even to something you love doing. It's so much easier to act like you don't care. People are embarrassed to be seen to fail. I grew tired of that attitude a few years ago, it feels so damaging and negative. Come out and be proud of what you are, what you're doing, who you want to be. Why not? Why act like you don't care when you do. Why let people think you're drifting through this instead of fighting through. You never know, it may just be the best thing you do.

Maybe it's a big city thing. Once we moved down to the South West, I took up the baton stronger than ever. Probably because each rehearsal was a seven-hour round trip. If I was going to carry on, I was really going to carry on. Also, when hanging out at the Dropout Studio or at shows I've always felt a little bit like the straight-laced person. The parent. The one making sure things didn't go too off the hook. Now, having not drunk for six years and not eaten meat for over twenty years and basically being boring as hell I really feel like I'm driving a lorry. I'm replacing the wheels while still driving, leaning out the cab and putting a wing mirror back on, patching up a rusty hole, still holding the road at 70mph. You think being in a big city will be inspiring. You think you're surrounding yourself with the best people. It's not until you move away and you surround yourself with yourself. You are your own inspiration. The city is full of reasons not to do things. Being bored is hugely under rated, a lot can come from it.

The band was never going to end when Tim left. It was never going to end when Jon left. Or James, or Ian, or Duncan, or when Rhys left for a year, or when the other two Tim's quit. It will do, one day. But not just yet. We'll know when to stop.

Within weeks of Tim leaving, Roo and I were getting together in his loft. This wasn't a wake. It was an opportunity for Roo and I, for the others, to prove ourselves. Paul's vocals have improved so much over the last couple of years. We planned to write songs that he could really open up on. We discussed where we wanted to go and what we wanted to do.

'Cleaner 1, Rough Mix' is currently my favourite song of the new batch. It is, you may be surprised to hear, not actually going to be called that. This song may not even make it onto the next record. It's amongst fourteen other songs we've recorded and we're just now, on the 5th May 2018, looking at booking another weekend in the studio. Maybe in June. We have no band-related activity in June. We have all the shows through May and Henry Blacker have two shows, one with Pere Ubu in London and another in Bristol with Ho9909. May is busy. June is looking welcoming, we're desperate to get back on the case with the new record. There's a chance we'll get another five or six down. 'Cleaner 1, Rough Mix' could end up not making the cut.

This is one of the tunes I played to Elisa when the rough mixes came through a couple of months ago. I believe it was tears of relief as opposed to tears of amazement at the quality of the song, but she cried none the less. She could rest easy, I wasn't about to do the spiralling now that Tim had bailed. In fact, things couldn't be further from the truth. We had a fresh and fired up optimism. Change is healthy. Don't fear change. This is a self-help book. Take my word for it, change is good. Move on. Don't wait. Sort your own life.

The song starts with Roo and Leon playing a spidery jerky guitar part. Rhys and I come in after eight loops with what, at the moment, sounds like the most thundering and simple three-note rhythm splat. Paul's vocals join in. Paul is on fire. It's so nice to have melody over what the instruments are doing, it's very under rated is melody. Bob missed the recording of this song, he couldn't make it down until the Saturday. This was recorded the night before. He had to overdub his guitar with me sitting next to him counting the changes and helping with the structure, not that I knew it too well. We work quick. If you miss a day you miss three songs and you're playing catch up.

When you have a song that you're happy with it's hard to keep it under wraps. We haven't even been playing the new tunes live. I would argue that four or maybe five could easily slip straight into a set. We're holding them back though, we want to be 100 per cent. When the new record arrives, we want the songs to be fresh. Fresh for anyone watching, fresh for us.

Each new record we do we try and alter the way we go about the songwriting, we attempt to move with what we're listening to, we want new things to influence. Progress. This song is that. Most of the new songs are more direct, a direct energy with direct attack. They're not harsh punk songs or brutal death metal but they are direct. The vocal is running things. Those of us in the band who are playing instruments like to play the correct notes, we don't need to be going crazy. We don't need to be climbing up monitors and jumping around. No one is watching us. Everyone is watching the frontman. Every band who has a front person is hiding behind that person. That person is leading the charge. No one in the crowd is staring at the bass player or the drummer. It's perfect for those of us who are playing the notes. The new songs are being created, as interestingly as we can, as open season for the vocals. To relate it to football, the bass and drums are the back line. The guitars are the midfield. The vocals are up front. How is the team set out, what tactics you use, it's up to you. Will all the guitars play high notes, do you have a creative midfield? Does the bass keep it simple and smack it into Row Z or is it more likely to try and play it out from the back with some fiddly, risky manoeuvres?

We've ironically been lucky that we've never achieved any

massive success. We all like creating music. If at any point we'd got big we possibly would have felt obliged to stick with the winning format. But, and to repeat myself, bands who stick with the same sound album after album are lying to you. They're doing it because it's what got them success. They're scared of progress. Very few bands change sound and keep their success. We like moving. We like releasing something that makes the few people that like us scratch their heads. It's harder for those discovering us new and working back through the discography than those who have stuck with us and kept up with the changes. If your entry point is *Radio Static High* and you go back to *Project:Death* you are going to be left confused. They are different bands. Keeping the same name from 2003 up to now is foolhardy. Stick with it, it'll be worth it.

The Guillotine was a darker record, covering the times around 2016 and 2017. Trump, UK politics, race, equality issues. We felt hopeless. The album was darker than the previous two, more minor key. The set up was the same though, and the same set up has remained for what will be our new record. Leon, Roo, Rhys, Paul, Bob, me. Will is now beginning to rehearse with us to cover Leon who can't always get out of work. Could we end up with four guitarists and one bass? We may need two conductors. It's progress.

I have different recordings of this song, marking out its development. From Roo and I jamming in his loft, to the group working it out and putting it all in order, to the current rough mix version. It's hard talking about this process with most people, so I hope you, the reader, if you've got this far, will grant me a minute more to blither. You don't need to be a professional musician to act professionally towards the music you make. Maybe one day vast amounts of people will get into your sounds but more than likely they won't. We don't stress. With a song like this one, where we've put hours into creating it and rehearsing it and driving to sessions and recording, it gets to the point where you almost don't care about anything other than the end result. I want a CDR for the car, so I can listen at 5.55am on my drive to work. At forty-four-years-old I think I've gone over the bridge and will now not stop making music, even if it's hopeless solo stuff that no one hears. Ideally, I want to keep playing music with other people. It's an easy way to communicate without talking. Going from loft jam, to rehearsal tape, to final recording is still, to me, an incredible way to work. Seeing the workings.

Elisa, Freddie, Stan and I have just got off the computer phone. We were seeing and talking to my brother Chris, his wife Maggie and their almost five-year-old son Luc. They are still in Brisbane. They've been there now for fifteen years, since the end of Stanton. I miss them. I hope it's not just me that thinks like this, but I find when I don't speak to people who I miss, I miss them less. They're not at the forefront of my mind. I hate saying goodbye when we meet. We've been to Australia twice and they've been over here two or three times. Saying goodbye is brutal. We're not here on earth long enough to be apart for too long, yet we're not here short enough to be in each other's pockets all the time. We all have our own life. To remind all, but mainly myself: When you're on holiday for a week or two in a distant land that is not life, that is holiday. If you lived there you would have to work, pay bills, deal with bastard neighbours. You would end up doing what you do now, not leaving the house, watching a series on your laptop, sniffing the milk to see if it has another day. The grass is not greener on the other side, it's not particularly green anywhere. Don't kid yourself. Make your patch work for you, put some cricket stumps on it, put a barbecue on it, whatever, make it your own thing.

Since getting back from the Sumac dates we're all now utterly focused on the new record. It's been a long time since we started working on it.

Overdub sessions are being booked, Paul will re-do some vocals in London, we have decided on a track list for the album. The kitty is filling back up after the recent tour, we have the money to cover all rehearsals and recordings. Will is going to add some guitar parts in Bristol. Our long- time friend and regular appearance-maker in this book, Chris from Grey Hairs, is adding some guitar and sending it down from Nottingham. Leon's parts are nice though. Who knows, some of the album will have five guitar parts on. Roo is maybe looking at adding some synth or keyboards. We're getting Daniel, from Grumbling Fur/Miracle/This Is Not This Heat, to add some violin and clarinet and recorder. He'll do this at home and send the parts over. We have a self-created deadline of August to be finished.

Will is now 100% in the band, Leon has left. Chris is in. He has replaced Roo who is now holed up in a loft with brother Tim creating a new Reigns record. We are now sadly Farthing-less. The revolving door may now be locked tight for a while.

Alter are going to release it. Alter release some of our favourite music, like Bass Clef, Total Control, Liberez, and Hieroglyphic Being. The label is run by Luke Younger who is the bass player in The Lowest Form and creates solo records under the name Helm. He was in The!Lights!Alive!, if you remember them from thousands of words ago. It's a small world.

I quite fancy two albums for 2019 but when I suggested it to Rhys he replied: "I like the idea of three."

We have some work to do.

This book is about the songs. The songs are nothing without the life going on around them. The delays through work, near family, distant family, illness, death, birth, marriage, honeymoons, touring, band members leaving. The inspiration those things give. We've released eleven albums in fifteen years. It will soon be twelve in sixteen. One day, when we're staring at the final star we'll see, this whole storm will barely register. It will have been a blip in our lives. A thousand punctuations marking our existence. We had a child. We played for forty minutes in Istanbul. We worked as a postman for years and years. We played twenty-five minutes in Valencia. We got married. We released a split seven-inch with The Phil Collins Three. I still want the new record to be called *Carnival.* No one else does.

Line-up timeline for Hey Colossus
2003–2019

On the off-chance you can't follow the story. On the off-chance the fact that we've been through three Tim's and two Farthings. On the off-chance that three people have come and gone and come back again. On the off-chance you worry about all this and would like some clarification, here is the fully fact-checked list of comings and goings. Only included are the instruments that were played live. If I included the studio instruments as well it would get messy.

Bob Davis, guitar/vocals, 2003 to present day
Joe Thompson, bass, 2003 to present day
Tim Hall, drums, 2003 – 2006
Ian Scanlon, guitar/vocals, 2003 - 2006
James Parker, guitar/vocals, 2003 – 2008
Rhys Llewellyn, drums 2006 – 2011 / 2013 to present day
Dave Briggs, guitar, 2006 – 2006
Duncan Brown, cosmic leader, 2006 – 2013 (on and off)
Tim Farthing, guitar/vocals 2008 – 2017
Paul Sykes, vocals/boxes of noise 2008 to present day
Will Saunders, guitar, 2009 – one show as cover, in Newport.
Jonathan Richards, guitar, 2010 – 2016
Leon Marks, synth/guitar, 2010 – 2013 / 2017 – 2018
Tim Cedar, drums, 2011 – 2013
Roo Farthing, guitar, 2016 – 2018
Will Pearce, guitar, 2018 to present day
Chris Summerlin, 2018 to present day

Thanks and Credits

The front cover photo was taken by Freddie Thompson early one Sunday morning in our garden.

Thanks to Elisa, Stan, Freddie – for putting up with me hunched over a £120 laptop at the kitchen table surrounded by full then empty then full cups, Sunday after Sunday. Shouting at my inept sausage fingers crashing away hopelessly, missing the target endlessly. Headphones on.

Okay, big and hearty cheers to everyone else in the HC band, past, present and future. Teamwork has got us to this lofty position, one day we'll all look back and cry.

The labels who have helped release our sounds. The bands who have influenced and hung with us. The venues for battling to stay open. The decent promoters out there. The splendid folk who turn up and watch the music and buy the records. Those who I spoke too for this book.

Kathy Young. Elisa's mum, Stan and Freddie's gran. For endless amounts of baby-sitting in the early days.

Dad. Mending amps. Looking after boys.

The mighty Earl Grey for his tea. Some say you taste of soap I think you're like lukewarm bath water, shared bath water, second body into mucky bathwater, just like we did in the 1970s and early 1980s. Then we got a shower and ruined it / finally got clean, depending on your viewpoint. Earl Grey is a flashback to the good times drink.

The Quietus for making me write the piece that you skipped at the beginning of the book, and then Mark Hodkinson of Pomona for reading it from their website and getting in touch, and Geoff Read for his patience and layout skills.

Penultimately, I want to thank the inventor of music, he or she totally nailed it.

And, if you've got this far, you.

> *Top tip:* Instrumental music is easier to write too. A few favourites being Tin Man, Clams Casino, Macintosh Plus (I ordered this record, it never showed up, the label never replied, I'm still in tears), Bob James *One* and Carl Craig's *Landcruising* album.

By the way, #np *the feed-back*. On this record it's the drums. They're working full time, they're doing all the heavy lifting.

The album is called *the feed-back*. The artist is either The Group or the feed-back depending on where you look. The band is more famously known as Gruppo di Improvvisazione Nuova Consonanza, this was a one off break away from that moniker. They are from Italy.

You need to know this came out in 1970 and it'd cost you hundreds of pounds to dig up an original. You need to also know I don't care about owning original pressings, so when a repress drops, and it comes with a CD for the van, and the press and remaster is spot on, and for added points it has an Obi strip, then I'm IN. Schema/RCA Italiana, back in 2014, did the do on this and you should find a copy as one day it'll be back up in the triple figures. I just want the music on a physical format. Once it becomes a rare vinyl nerd-off, I'm outta there. Of course, right now I'm listening on YouTube. But I have the record, I'm content. I've done my bit.

We have a new dog. His name is Monty. He does a lot of sniffing and pissing. He has no love for our socks, he wants them off our feet. When you watch a new-to-this-world creature discovering its surroundings it's an alluring sight. The TV goes off, the family reunites in a pre-demise of civilization round the fire-place way. Staring at this new thing as it dances its wobbly dance, tip toeing on grass, skidding on damp decking. We're staring at fire like it's the best thing ever, and it is. Computer phones are packed away, the TV is off, and as we chuckle together we're a unit regrouping.

The feed-back's record, featuring on trumpet a certain Ennio Morricone, clocks in at 28 minutes. It has three tunes and sits perfectly on a single LP. It derives all its feel, swing, funk, and drive from the drums. The drums are recorded so well. The drums are doing what good drums do, they anchor it. They are the house. The oven. The stereo. Your bed. They are the importants. The things your world needs, the bass drum, the high hat, the snare. A band is only as good as it's drummer, and this cat, Renzo Restuccia, is clearly one of the greats.

Everything else on this record is the new dog.

There are six other people on these tracks pulling your socks off, pissing on your carpet, chewing floor scraps. They are trying to ruin the house whilst the drums chase them through the building. Aggro always unites the world. Aggro is the modern day fire place, the world huddles around a commotion, rubbing it's hands. There's piano, guitar, bass, trombone, vocal noises, Ennio's brass, more percussion, and much else besides. They're tearing the place apart, they can all play like hell. Today I'll listen and only hear the drums, tomorrow it'll be the six other characters, the day after it'll be all together. This album is a house that's come to life, it's gone from grey to technicolour, the rooms are blaring.

I got great love for this record. I would put money on hip hop heads digging the hell out of the beats while their younger avant garde sister is getting off on the blasts emanating from the rest of the Italian crew. I am both the hip hop head and the younger sister.

Think 'Tony Conrad scraping over him from Can on the tubs.' Think 'Sunburned Hand losing it over Mr. Clyde Stubblefield.' Or don't think at all, get this record and be over the moon that you can come up with your own dream team of rhythm and sound. Let it make you wish you were in the room when it was recorded, watching the dog destroy your world, watching it bring your world together.

So, Mum, does it in any way make sense now?

I think I'm more confused

ALSO PUBLISHED BY POMONA

Trevor Hoyle
RULE OF NIGHT
DOWN THE FIGURE 7

Boff Whalley
FOOTNOTE*

Hunter Davies
THE FAN
MEAN WITH MONEY
THE SECOND HALF

Crass
LOVE SONGS

Bill Nelson
DIARY OF A HYPERDREAMER VOLUME 1
DIARY OF A HYPERDREAMER, VOL 2

Fred Eyre
KICKED INTO TOUCH

Barry Hines
LOOKS AND SMILES
THE PRICE OF COAL
THIS ARTISTIC LIFE

Clancy Sigal
ZONE OF THE INTERIOR

Christopher Barker
THE ARMS OF THE INFINITE

Mark Hodkinson
THAT SUMMER FEELING
THE LAST MAD SURGE OF YOUTH
BELIEVE IN THE SIGN

Simon Armitage
THE NOT DEAD

Ian McMillan & Martyn Wiley
THE RICHARD MATTHEWMAN STORIES

Kenneth Slawenski
JD SALINGER: A LIFE RAISED HIGH

Esther Fairfax
MY IMPROPER MOTHER AND ME

Catherine Smyth
WEIRDO. MOSHER. FREAK.
The Murder of Sophie Lancaster

Stuart Murdoch
THE CELESTIAL CAFÉ

Simon Armitage
 BLACK ROSES: THE KILLING OF SOPHIE LANCASTER

Dale Hibbert
BOY INTERRUPTED

Bob Stanley
SLEEVENOTES